DOING LIFE WITH GOD 2

by

Bo Boshers

with Kim Anderson

 LOVELAND, COLORADO

D0109378

Group's R.E.A.L. Guarantee to you:

Every Group resource incorporates our R.E.A.L. approach to ministry—a unique philosophy that results in long-term retention and life transformation. It's ministry that's:

R **E** **A** **L**

Relational
Because student-to-student interaction enhances learning and builds Christian friendships.

Experiential
Because what students experience sticks with them up to 9 times longer than what they simply hear or read.

Applicable
Because the aim of Christian education is to be both hearers and doers of the Word.

Learner-based
Because students learn more and retain it longer when the process is designed according to how they learn best.

Doing Life With God 2

Credits

Editor: Amy Simpson

Creative Development Editor: Jim Kochenburger

Chief Creative Officer: Joani Schultz

Copy Editor: Betty Taylor

Designer and Art Director: Jean Bruns

Computer Graphic Artist: Joyce Douglas

Illustrator: Dave Bramsen

Cover Art Director: Jeff Storm

Production Manager: Dodie Tipton

ISBN 0-7644-2228-6

10 9 8 7 6 5 4 3 2 1   10 09 08 07 06 05 04 03 02 01

Printed in the United States of America.

Acknowledgments

The thirty devotions in this book are real-life stories of Christian students doing life with God and how they found his power to deal with a variety of situations. I am grateful for their honesty and willingness to share their stories.

I'd also like to thank the youth ministers who helped find students interested in participating in this project. They serve in the following churches around the world: Coast Hills Community Church, Aliso Viejo, California; North Ridge Community Church, Phoenix, Arizona; Heart of the Springs Baptist Church, Colorado Springs, Colorado; Willow Creek Community Church, South Barrington, Illinois; Lakeside Church, Guelph, Ontario, Canada; Shire Christian Centre, Sutherland, Australia; Basileia Vineyard, Basel, Switzerland; Crossings Community Church, Oklahoma City, Oklahoma; Santa Cruz Bible Church, Santa Cruz, California; Valley Christian Center, Dublin, California; Grace Community Church, Houston, Texas; Corvallis Church of the Nazarene, Corvallis, Oregon; Memorial Baptist Church, Evansville, Indiana; St. Andrew's Church, Oxford, United Kingdom; First United Methodist Church of Oviedo, Oviedo, Florida; and Fellowship Church, Grapevine, Texas.

In addition to the students and churches listed above, I'm thankful for the Willow Creek Association and for president Jim Mellado's vision and leadership, for Doug Yonamine's willingness to answer all of my questions; and Christine Anderson for your giftedness and all that you do—it's a joy to work with you.

Group Publishing is committed to making quality resources available for students. Thanks to Amy Simpson, Kelli Trujillo, and the rest of the Group team for the work all of you did to make this book a reality.

Melissa D'Alexander once again helped keep the material relevant and focused on God's Word. Emily Bell provided creative writing, and I'm thankful our paths crossed so unexpectedly. Thanks to both of you for faithfully using your gifts to help students become fully devoted to Christ.

Thanks to my good friend Kim Anderson, who once again makes my weaknesses look like strengths. Without your patience, organization, and creativity, this project would not have been possible.

And to my three wonderful kids: Brandon, Tiffany, and Trevor. I am so proud to be your father. Thanks for all your help and prayers. I love you.

To my wife and best friend, Gloria. You are an awesome example of God's love to me. Thank you, Gloria, for twenty-one awesome years of marriage! I love you!

4

Contents

Social Life

Introduction

• Jenna has taken a stand against drinking. How does God help her stay strong?

• Steve's worried about his future. How does he remember that God has a perfect plan for his life?

• Christy's friend is pregnant and considering an abortion. How does Christy support her friend during this crisis?

• Connor's dad is an alcoholic. How has Connor handled a difficult home life?

You'll find out exactly how Jenna, Steve, Christy, and Connor handled these real-life situations because their stories (and twenty-six other student stories) are included in this book. The guys and girls who contributed to this book face many of the same challenges you do as a Christian teenager. They understand how hard it can be to fit in, make choices that honor God, get along with parents and siblings, and grow spiritually. Sometimes you may feel as if you're all alone in trying to figure out life, but be encouraged and know that you are not alone!

How to Use This Devotional

You may have read devotionals that are organized by specific dates. You turn to the devotion for a particular day, hoping for words of encouragement. But what if that devotion doesn't apply at all to what you're dealing with at that moment? It can be discouraging and cause you to lose interest.

The devotions in this book are organized in four main sections. You can find issues that you or a friend may be facing and read about other students who went through similar situations. Or you can choose your own daily devotion to encourage and remind you of God's love and awesome power. Each devotion is written to help you learn life lessons through the choices (some good, some bad) made by other Christian students.

Here are the four main sections in *Doing Life With God 2*:

• **Private Life**—the private areas in your life that challenge and strengthen your character

• **Spiritual Life**—doing life with God and growing in your faith

• **Home Life**—relating to family members in ways that honor God

• **Social Life**—the issues you face with peers

Each devotion includes the following elements:

• **A Student's Story**—a story about God working in a student's life

• **What God Taught Me**—powerful lessons God taught the student and key Bible verses for you to study

• **Write Your Story**—a chance for you to reflect on your own story and write your thoughts through a journal exercise

• **Talk to God**—a suggested prayer you can use to talk to God

• **Talk With Friends**—three questions related to the story for you to discuss with a few friends or in a small-group setting

Connecting with God by reading a devotion each day will deepen your personal relationship with him and give you wisdom and strength to face each day.

As you read this book, you may feel that you have a story that needs to be told. Well, if that's the case, send it in or e-mail it! The addresses are in the back of the book on page 95. It would be great to read your story and hear how God is at work in your life.

My prayer is that these devotions will give you hope, inspiration, and encouragement to keep you strong with God each day. Remember, being a Christian is awesome, and other Christian students around the world face similar situations. You aren't alone—keep fighting the good fight, dream big for God, and be a difference-maker today.

PRIVATE LIFE

Time to Pay Attention

Heather's Story

The week had been a rough one for me, full of disappointments and regrets. Every morning I woke up and dreaded what the day held for me. But I was still psyched to go to my student ministry and worship with friends. In fact, it was the only thing I had looked forward to all week.

Just before I was going to leave, my mom walked into my room and started yelling at me. We got into it for about ten minutes, and I ended the conversation by saying I had to go do better things. I was so sick of our daily fights. After she left my room, I packed my backpack for church with the usual: my Bible, a couple of pens, and a pad of paper. But I decided to also add a knife.

> "For you created my inmost being; you knit me together in my mother's womb. I praise you because I am fearfully and wonderfully made; your works are wonderful, I know that full well" (Psalm 139:13-14).

I sometimes used self-mutilation as a way out. I don't know why, but it made me feel better—especially after a fight with my mom. But after my week at school and the fight with my mom, this time I wanted more than a gash in my leg or a scar on my hand. I wanted out permanently. I wanted to die.

I tried to concentrate during the service, but my mind kept wandering back to my knife. It was comforting to know it was there. My knife was my ticket out, should I need it. The knife consumed my thoughts. When could I use it? Where could I go to use it? What part of me could I hurt?

At one point during the service, I quickly slipped away to the bathroom,

*pulled the knife out of my backpack, and cut a deep gash in my wrist. I
thought I was alone in that bathroom, but I wasn't. God was there with me.*

*I went back into the service like nothing had happened. I was crying
and hiding my wrist. I thought I would feel better, but I only felt embar-
rassed. No one would understand this! I was standing near my friend Rachel.
It didn't take her long to notice my tears...and my wrist. She asked me what
was wrong, but I couldn't speak, so instead I showed her. I was so ashamed!
Rachel led me back to the bathroom and grabbed some paper towels to stop
the bleeding. A few other girls in the bathroom just stared and then left to
go find a leader to help. Just what I needed. They'd probably call my
parents and put me in a psych ward. What I thought would bring peace had
only brought more strife.*

*I wanted to hide or run. I just wanted to get out of there. But in that
moment, two people had a hold of me, Rachel and Jesus. I wasn't going anywhere. In a far corner of my heart, I felt a still, small voice trying to comfort me. But I didn't want it to comfort me. I wanted to feel my pain.*

*Eventually I ended up on the bathroom floor under the sinks. I couldn't
even move. I just wanted to keep crying. Todd, an adult leader, came into
the bathroom to try to talk to me. There I was on the bathroom floor, under the sinks, with a gashed wrist and a broken heart. Someone wanted to
help me? I didn't think it was possible.*

*I finally came out from under the sinks and got a ride home from
Rachel. My parents got the phone call, and I had a long talk with them when
I got home. That still, small voice in the corner of my heart grew to a large
booming voice. God was trying to talk to me! It was time to listen and pay
attention.*

What God Taught Me

• When I feel down, I should talk with my parents and not pull away
from them. Being suicidal is a very serious issue. If you or someone you love
is thinking about suicide, get help fast!

• God created me and feels my pain when I'm hurting. Jesus wants to
carry my burdens and walk with me through life's challenges.

• God loves to hear my prayers. I can talk with him every day about
everything going on in my life.

• God has placed others in my life to comfort, counsel, and pray for me.

Write Your Story

God, thank you for giving me the strength and courage to overcome...

Talk to God

Use this prayer, or talk to God in your own words:

Jesus, thank you for never giving up on me. When I don't like myself very well, I know you love me so much and unconditionally. I praise you that I am fearfully and wonderfully made. Help me not to forget that I'm your precious, beloved child. Amen.

Talk With Friends

In a small group, talk about these questions:

• If a friend came to you or if you heard about a friend who was talking about suicide, what would you say or do for him or her?

• What advice does the Bible give us about dealing with difficult times? How has this advice helped you in the past?

• What stops you from listening to God's counsel?

A Total 180

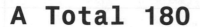

Caroline's Story

Growing up, I hated church—absolutely hated going. I had no friends there, and I was the only one who didn't know all the books in the Bible. But most of all, I hated having to wear a dress every Sunday. Each week, I would fake being sick or try to sleep in late so I wouldn't have to go, but my mom always found a way to get me to church.

I grew up thinking church held no important place in my life and neither did God. When I was in fourth grade, my parents got a divorce, and a year later my dad moved to a different state. After the divorce, my whole family started fighting—my mom and dad couldn't get along, my two sisters and I hated each other, and all three of us fought with our parents.

We continued to go to church, but I began to outsmart my mom. Instead of going to Sunday school, my friend Jennifer and I walked around the neighborhood that surrounded the church. I did this for over a year, until my mom finally caught me. Eventually, we stopped going on a weekly basis. What a relief!

Jennifer and I weren't a good influence on each other. We began shoplifting on a regular basis, often walking out of a mall with hundreds of dollars worth of shoes, clothes, CDs, and makeup. It became addicting. I knew in my heart that what we were doing was wrong, but I continued to do it anyway.

During this time, I could not believe in God. I suffered from depression and on certain days just felt like dying. One night when I was visiting my dad, I was so unhappy with my life and with myself that I went outside in the middle of a huge lightning storm and sat against a tall metal pole, hoping a bolt would strike it and put me out of my misery.

I had stopped believing in God because I was angry at this "loving God" for making my life so miserable. My life continued to go further downhill. I began drinking regularly to numb my pain. Being involved in the party scene made the situation with my family and my mixed-up beliefs even worse. I was lying and fighting with them all the time. I knew I was heading in the wrong direction, but I didn't know how to turn my life around.

The summer before my sophomore year, I started dating a guy named Jeff. We were complete opposites—I'm still amazed we ever got together!

He came from a strong Christian home. He had strong morals and wasn't into the party scene. My home life was still pretty messed up, and I was a total partier. The longer we went out, the more he influenced my life and the decisions I was making. Being around Jeff's family also had a powerful effect on me. His parents and I developed an awesome relationship; they're like my second parents. I began to desire the close relationship Jeff had with his parents and his sisters. I began looking for that kind of peace and happiness for my own life.

"Do not be misled: 'Bad company corrupts good character'" (1 Corinthians 15:33).

After a few months of dating Jeff, I stopped drinking and left the party scene completely. I started going with him to Fellowship of Christian Athletes (FCA) meetings at my school. One night, a girl talked about her personal relationship with Jesus and the important role he played in her life. After hearing and seeing how happy she was, I knew that only God could turn my life around.

I didn't accept Jesus Christ in my heart that night, but I continued to ask questions and look for answers. I didn't feel quite ready to make the commitment because I was scared God wouldn't forgive me for my sins. I wanted God's love, but I felt he could not love me because of all the wrong things I had done.

During summer vacation, I was invited to go on a trip with Jeff's family. We met up with another family whose son Troy was best friends with Jeff. Troy had always influenced me in seeking God because his faith was so strong. He lived his life with integrity and did not compromise his beliefs.

One night during our trip, I knew I wanted God in my life, but I didn't know how or what to ask him. Troy and I went on a walk, and he told me a lot about his faith and explained to me how to become a Christian. Two hours later, I accepted Jesus Christ into my heart. I felt free! After that night, my life turned a radical 180.

My relationship with my family has improved so much. My sisters and I are now civil to each other, and I was finally able to say "I love you" to my dad (which I hadn't said to him in over four years). All the anger and bitterness I had toward him was gone. God turned my family life around.

I began looking for a church to attend. A teacher at school suggested the church she attended. The first Sunday I went, I felt welcome and accepted. After becoming a Christian, I knew my group of friends had to *change and I needed a few Christian friends who would help me grow in my new faith. I had to remove myself from the group of friends I had hung out with for over two years. Several people were mad at me, but I knew what I was doing was right.*

For the first time ever, I am satisfied with my life. I am finally happy, by the grace of God. I am thankful that God placed other people in my life to point me toward a personal relationship with God and turn my life around.

What God Taught Me

• God is faithful. He never gave up on me, even when I turned away from him.

• Christian friends are important. They help me stay on track spiritually and encourage me to make good choices. It's also important to be involved in a church to get connected and receive Bible teaching.

• God promises in Matthew 7:7-8 that if we seek him, we will find him.

Write Your Story

What friend could you share your faith with and point toward God? Write that friend's name, and ask God to use you to make a difference in that friend's life.

Talk to God

Use this prayer, or talk to God in your own words:

Jesus, thank you for being faithful to me and for being a God of second chances. Forgive me for the times I've walked away from you and made poor choices. Use me to influence my friends and point them toward you. Amen.

Talk With Friends

In a small group, talk about these questions:

• Are your friends pointing you toward or away from God? Are you hanging out with good company or bad company? (See the verse on page 13.)

• When have you felt far from God? What helped draw you closer to him? What keeps you close to God?

• How can we help one another to be examples of God's love to our non-Christian friends?

Taking Off the Masks
Julia's Story

We all wear masks from time to time. We try to cover up how we really feel by pretending to be someone else. We act as if life is great when really we feel like giving up on it. We smile and appear energetic when really all we want to do is stay in bed so we don't have to face the world. We may even encourage other people and act hyper in an attempt to hide what's happening in our hearts.

Not long ago, I wasn't being real with my feelings. I hated life and felt totally alone, yet I wouldn't let anyone in on my pain. At home, I put on the mask of busyness so there would never be enough time for anyone to question me about me. I always had somewhere to go, someone to talk to, or homework to do. This disguise protected me from having to share with my parents or siblings even the slightest detail of what my days were really like.

At school, I put on the mask of happiness and caring for other people. If I cared for other people, no one would even think to ask about me. I didn't want anyone to know the real Julia. The real Julia was tired, in a state of hopelessness, and despairing. I worked hard to hide that side of myself so everyone saw the fun, caring Julia. It worked—no one suspected a thing.

Deep down, I wanted someone to reach out to me, to tell me that everything would be OK, to pray with me, and to care for me, but I had done such a good job of perfecting my masks that no one even knew there was a problem. If I let others see the real me, everyone would know I wasn't pulled together and always happy. But I knew if I continued to wear the masks, I would blow up. I needed a new start so I wouldn't have to be fake and I could sort things out.

One day I decided to run away. But I didn't get very far. My older brother figured out my plans and called a youth pastor from a local church to pray for me and meet with me. But how could this youth pastor help me and understand my messed-up life?

For some reason, I decided to go to church the next Sunday. Ron, the youth pastor who had prayed for me, asked if we could hang out that after-noon. I figured it couldn't hurt, so I said yes. When we got together, I real-ized it was easy to talk to Ron. I felt like he really listened and cared about me. I couldn't believe I even told him the horrible secret of my suicide attempt a couple of years earlier.

"My soul finds rest in God alone; my salvation comes from him. He alone is my rock and my salva-tion; he is my fortress, I will never be shaken" (Psalm 62:1-2).

I had worked so hard to make my masks hide the real me, but I had forgotten about God. Even if I had fooled everyone else, I couldn't fool God. He didn't see the hyper, busy girl everyone else did. He didn't even see the outside appearance I had worked so hard on. He saw my heart. He knew all my pain, my sadness, and my despair. The Bible says God even knows every tear I have ever cried. And when I thought no one was reaching out to me, his mighty hand was on my shoulder. God knew what I needed and allowed my brother to see through my disguise. There is no mask that will hide you from God's love.

I am convinced that God brought Ron into my life at just the right time. He continued to support me and remind me how much God loves me. I knew I needed God in my life, so eventually I trusted him with all my heart.

I have started to show people who I really am, and it feels good. I still wrestle with depression and sometimes try to cover it up. But I have learned that I can't hide from my heavenly Father. He sees behind my masks and helps me take them off, one by one.

What God Taught Me

• God has given me strength, people to support me, and his unconditional love. God has healed so much of the pain I carried around for so long. When I fall back into depression, I look to God's power and to the wisdom in the Bible.

• It hasn't been an easy process, but God has taught me that he is and always will be available to help me when I call on him.

• God taught me how important it is to have people in my life I can talk with honestly and who will encourage and pray for me.

Write Your Story

What mask do you hide behind? Ask God to help you see yourself as he sees you. Remember, you are his beloved.

Talk to God

Use this prayer, or talk to God in your own words:

Jesus, you are my rock; you are stable and secure. I know I can count on you to walk through life with me, each step of the way. Teach me to depend on you for all things. My strength comes from you and I am grateful. Amen.

Talk With Friends

In a small group, talk about these questions:

• Why do people wear masks to hide their true feelings? How can knowing God help you remove masks?

• How does God's love give you confidence to be yourself? What causes you to forget this truth and to hide behind a mask?

• How could the members of this group help one another feel more accepted and free to be themselves?

A New Start

Katie's Story

At the end of my eighth-grade year, my parents decided to move. It wasn't the first move I had made; it was the fifth! I dreaded moving again. I had so many close friends I would have to say goodbye to and plans I would have to leave behind. After moving so much, I had grown very shy and self-conscious. A friend said to me, "Katie, every time we do anything, you're so quiet and you never voice your opinion. We can't know what you like or want if you don't tell us."

That one statement had a huge impact on my life. I had always dreamed about making a difference for God by sharing my faith. Without knowing it, my friend helped me see that I was never going to make that difference if I didn't open up and start talking.

I had always wanted to be an outgoing leader on my high school campus, and I knew I had it in me. Since I was starting a new school, I decided to turn over a new leaf. I wasn't going to be shy anymore. I knew it wasn't going to be easy, but I also knew that God would be by my side.

"I can do everything through him who gives me strength" (Philippians 4:13).

I entered my new school with a completely different attitude. I felt like a different person. It was amazing what God did! He helped me make new friends quickly, and I even got involved in a student ministry at church. I also got the opportunity to talk to some of my friends, old and new, about Jesus!

I've been a Christian all my life, but when I turned my fears over to

*God so he could work through me, my whole perspective changed. He
showed me his love and I realized I'm someone special—his precious child.
Life isn't always easy, even with my attitude change. I still have days when
I want to shy away from others, but God has provided me with confidence
that comes only from him.*

What God Taught Me

• I have learned to trust God with every aspect of my life. He has helped
me grow in areas I didn't even realize I needed to grow.

• God has a purpose for my life. He'll lead me every step of the way.

• Prayer is powerful. I know I can talk to God throughout my day.

Write Your Story

This story highlights God's power and his ability to give us courage.
Where do you need God's help? Write a prayer request and let him know.

Talk to God

Use this prayer, or talk to God in your own words:

Jesus, I want you to take part in every area of my life. You have the perfect plan for my life. You open doors where I would never expect, and you bring people into my life I'd never dream of knowing. Please equip me with the confidence to depend on you for all things. Amen.

Talk With Friends

In a small group, talk about these questions:

• How do you think you'd react if you had to move as many times as Katie did? How would you handle so many new school environments?

• Do you know of a new student at your school who you could reach out to? What could you do or say to make that student feel welcome and accepted?

• What one change could you make in your Christian example at school? What might stop you from making this change?

Don't Give It Away

Kelly's Story

When I was fourteen years old and just starting high school, I was looking forward to my new classes. But instead of focusing on what was being taught in my classes, I dreamed about all the cute boys around me.

I'll never forget a weekend in February that impacted my life in a way I was unprepared for. It began when a friend and I went to McDonald's after a basketball game. When we sat down, I noticed a really good-looking guy had followed us. His name was Derek, and he had all my attention—and I had his.

I asked him to give me a ride to my friend's house. On the way there, he stopped and took me to a fraternity party on the local college campus. I was excited. He was so cute, and I knew something was going to happen! While we danced, I got closer and made the first move.

What began as a kiss turned into a heartache. Every move he made and every word he said made me feel secure, happy, and in love. After two days, I had sex with Derek and thought I had found the love of a lifetime.

But he didn't call me for a while or spend much time with me after our encounter. He wasn't as friendly as when we first met, but I was still infatuated with him. Even when I found out he'd also had sex with my best friend, I still wanted him to love me.

I guess I knew about the physical part of sex, but I was unaware of the emotional and spiritual disappointments to come later. I had lost the precious gift of purity. But sex felt so good—it became difficult for me to say no when put in other tempting situations.

One day after church, a lady I didn't know came up to me and began telling me a story. She asked me, "Do you really love your grandparents?"

"Yes," I replied.

She then said, "Well, suppose your grandma is really sick and is going to die. When she dies, she leaves you her diamond earrings. These are more precious to you than anything, and they're the only things to remember your grandma by. One day your boyfriend sees you wearing them and asks to wear one while you wear the other. What would you say?"

"No," I replied. "They mean the world to me."

The lady then said, "If you can say no to giving away those earrings, why can't you say no to giving away something as special and precious as your purity?"

At that moment, I saw God in her eyes and remembered I had prayed for God to help me resist sexual temptation. God had answered my prayers.

This encounter with a lady I didn't even know changed my views regarding sexuality. I began to learn from the Bible what a precious gift sex is within the boundaries of marriage and how easily I had been giving that gift away. I realized how wrong my actions had been the past couple of months and how much they must have grieved God. I asked for his forgiveness. I knew I needed to make many changes in my life. I needed a second chance, a clean slate, and I'm so grateful God erased all my sins. I am committed to not giving this valuable gift away again until I am married. With God's strength, I know I can do it.

> "Love is patient, love is kind. It does not envy, it does not boast, it is not proud. It is not rude, it is not self-seeking, it is not easily angered, it keeps no record of wrongs. Love does not delight in evil but rejoices with the truth. It always protects, always trusts, always hopes, always perseveres. Love never fails" (1 Corinthians 13:4-8a).

What God Taught Me

• God loves me with a love so much purer and deeper than any human ever could. He loves me unconditionally.

• God's Word gives wisdom about love and sex. His ways are the ones I want to follow the rest of my life—they are not restrictive, but life-giving.

• God taught me about forgiveness and how he is able to wash away my sins and make me pure again.

Write Your Story

It's so important to set boundaries before you find yourself in a tempting situation. In your dating life, what convictions and standards do you think God wants for you? Talk to him about it here, asking for wisdom and guidance.

Talk to God

Use this prayer, or talk to God in your own words:

Jesus, forgive me for the times I fail you and dishonor you with my

actions. Thank you for rescuing me from sin and giving me a fresh start.
Keep me on the right path so I can glorify you with my life. Amen.

Talk With Friends

In a small group, talk about these questions:

• Do you believe it's true that when God says "Wait," that should be
enough for us to know waiting is the right thing to do? Why or why not?

• If God is a God of second chances, why not have sex now and then
ask for forgiveness? (Read Romans 6:1-14.)

• What are some spiritual disciplines that help you stay pure? In what
ways do they help?

Soul Food

Lauren's Story

It seemed like I had it all: good grades at a Christian high school, nice
clothes, great parents, a personal relationship with God, and a supportive
church family. Other people thought I had it all together. But I didn't. I
was battling anorexia, and it was destroying my body and eating at my soul.

The struggle started when I watched television and read magazines.
Seeing all those perfect women in bathing suits and designer clothes caused
me to take a critical look at myself. Even watching the Miss America pageant
made me wish I weighed what the contestants did. Soon, everywhere I went,
all I could see were women with perfect bodies, perfect hair—perfect
everything. I wanted what they had. If only I looked like them, I thought,
my life would be glamorous and people would compliment me all the time.

Since my parents left for work early in the morning, it was easy for me
to skip breakfast. And because I was at school for lunch, it was pretty easy
to skip that meal too. As my disease progressed, so did the lies. I would tell
my friends I wasn't hungry because I'd had a huge breakfast. At dinner-
time, I would tell my parents I didn't want to eat because I'd had a large
lunch. I knew what I was doing was bad for my physical, spiritual, and
emotional well-being, but I didn't care. I had a goal to look a certain way,
and I was determined to make it happen!

I started to get really bad headaches when I wouldn't eat and even felt like I was going to faint a few times. My personality also started changing. When I didn't eat for a day, I would get really temperamental. Everything bothered me. And even though I was losing a lot of weight, I couldn't see a difference. I would look in the mirror and see parts of my body that were still fat and that needed work. I had to keep losing more weight! I was obsessed.

One Sunday at church, a youth leader I really respected talked about her struggle with an eating disorder. She described what her life was like during the struggle, and it was as if she were talking about me! She talked about how God helped her find the strength to start eating again and stop seeing herself as not good enough. In that moment, I knew I needed God's help too! I hadn't been very open with anyone before, but I decided I needed to talk to this leader. I confided in her, and she understood what I was going through. I no longer felt so alone.

Not only did she reassure me that I'm beautiful the way God made me, but she also prayed with me and taught me about what Jesus sees in me. He sees my heart, not my body. He cares about what my soul is up to, not what size skirt I fit into. I learned that I wasn't treating my body with respect and I needed to take better care of myself physically, spiritually, and emotionally.

"The Lord does not look at the things man looks at. Man looks at the outward appearance, but the Lord looks at the heart" (1 Samuel 16:7b).

I had never thought to involve God in this struggle, but this leader showed me the powerful role God had played in her recovery. Instead of admiring the beauty of Hollywood with its focus on outward appearances, I slowly started to concentrate on what was happening in my soul. God helped me shift my focus—to look at what really matters and has lasting value. For a long time, I had been neglecting my physical hunger, but I also realized my soul was hungry for God.

Even though I never got to the point of hospitalization or professional counseling, anorexia was and is a huge issue in my life. Each day is a struggle for me. Every morning, I have to remind myself that I'm beautiful the way God made me and renew my mind with truth from the Bible. I also have to eat every meal no matter what and ask God for help during the day to make the right food choices. My hunger for food—and for God—grows each day, and I'm grateful.

What God Taught Me

• My self-esteem needs to be rooted in God and what he thinks of me, not the images of television or magazines.

• Everything is possible with God. His power and strength can overcome any challenge I face.

• It's so important to be connected to the church and to speak up when I need help. God used my youth leader to help get me back on the right path and to get healthier emotionally, spiritually, and physically.

• Lying to my parents, my friends, God, and myself dug deeper holes for me to fall into—it was hard to get out. Being truthful is always the way to go.

Write Your Story

Have you been focusing more on your outward appearance than on your heart? Ask God to help you see yourself the way he sees you. Remember, you are precious in his sight.

Talk to God

Use this prayer, or talk to God in your own words:

Jesus, I'm thankful that my confidence comes from you and not from what other people think about me. Give me eyes to see myself as someone who is of great value to you. Thank you for reminding me that I am beautiful to you. Amen.

Talk With Friends

In a small group, talk about these questions:

• What would you do if a friend of yours was struggling with an eating disorder?

• Regarding your self-worth, what kind of messages do you get from the media? Do they help you feel better or worse? How is God's message different?

• Do you need to apologize to anyone for unkind words or jokes you've said about his or her appearance? What do you need to do to make it right?

What's Next, God?

Steve's Story

I've always wondered what God had planned for my future. What should I do for a living? Where should I live? Who will I marry? These were the questions I often asked myself. I felt like the years were flying by and I was going nowhere. I had no direction and no idea what I wanted to do with my life.

For a while, I thought being a doctor would be exciting and rewarding, but I didn't want to spend the next ten years in school. After that, I saw myself as a computer software programmer, but that didn't hold my interest. That's when I began to worry. With my average grades in school, I convinced myself I'd end up flipping burgers at McDonald's for the rest of my life. I worried that I wouldn't be able to afford a car or a house. I worried about who I would marry, then if I would get a divorce. I was freaking out about my whole future! For some reason, I thought I had to get it all figured out fast. Fortunately, God had it all under control.

At a youth convention, I realized all my stress over my future was really my lack of trust in God! I made a commitment to give him complete control of my future. I asked him to lead my life and use me in any way he wanted. Little did I know that God would take me on a new path in life that had me more involved than ever in my own church community. I began to help out with the junior high ministry and lead the high school worship time.

As my relationship with God grew, I began to see the direction my life was going to take. I knew God was calling me to full-time ministry. He gave me a passion for junior high students, and I plan to become a youth pastor.

With my career figured out, I moved on to worrying about my future spouse. What if I never got married because I couldn't find the right girl? Would God bring the right person to me? When? Who should I be looking for?

I confided in a Christian friend, who pointed me to some great Bible verses that talked about God's sovereignty and his awesome plan for each of us. I read those verses for a week, over and over again. I prayed that God would help me stop worrying and fully trust him.

> **"But seek first his kingdom and his righteousness, and all these things will be given to you as well. Therefore do not worry about tomorrow, for tomorrow will worry about itself. Each day has enough trouble of its own" (Matthew 6:33-34).**

I knew God's guidance and direction would lead me and help me figure out each step I should take. With the help of my good Christian friend and God's Word, I was, over time, able to tackle my problem of worrying and trust God with every area of my life.

What God Taught Me

• When I put my future in God's hands, he's able to work through me more effectively. Instead of spending so much energy worrying about the future, I can spend that energy serving him and others.

• I was being impatient with wanting to grow up so fast. I can see only what's before me and not what's to come. It's best to wait for God's perfect timing and not try to hurry things along.

• It's important to have Christian friends who hold me accountable and give me boosts of encouragement when I need it.

Write Your Story

Read Philippians 4:6. Are you anxious about anything? Tell God about it.

Talk to God

Use this prayer, or talk to God in your own words:

Jesus, you're strong and able to handle my burdens. I'm so glad I don't have to carry them by myself. I've learned that life is more joy-filled and peaceful when I depend on you for my future. Thank you for the guidance in my life so far. Help me remember to live one day at a time. Amen.

Talk With Friends

In a small group, talk about these questions:

• What would you like to be doing five years from now?

• Is it easy or difficult for you to give your future plans over to God? Why? What causes you to lose trust in God for your future?

• How do you see God using each group member's gifts and talents to make a difference? Spend some time as a group praying for one another, asking God to make your paths clear. Dream big!

SPIRITUAL LIFE

Always There

Matt's Story

I've grown up going to church and heard all the Bible stories. My mom and stepdad brought me to Sunday school every week during my elementary school years, but back then I was more into Super Mario Brothers than God. Church was just something we did each Sunday. After third grade, my family moved to a new house and we started attending a different church. I liked it right away.

The Sunday morning kids' program was very different from my old church—there was a live band and a message that really applied to my life. It was fun, but God still wasn't a significant factor in my life. Church was a good thing, but then I was more interested in basketball than in God. Yet my parents kept gently encouraging me to seek God and pointing me toward him.

My junior high years were very difficult. I felt out of place and alone at school. I had a couple of close friends and I was really active in sports, but I refused to just blindly follow my peers. I saw how my teammates and friends lived, and I didn't want to live that way. I kept searching for answers to my life questions. I didn't know it then, but God was there with me in the midst of my struggle, drawing me toward him. My parents also helped me on my spiritual journey by being examples to me of how a Christian should live.

Early in my freshman year of high school, my parents encouraged me to go to a Fellowship of Christian Athletes (FCA) meeting at my school. At the first meeting, I was shocked to see a dozen or so students I already knew. A teacher I respected spoke to us about Jesus, and I hung on every word.

At this FCA meeting, Jesus truly spoke directly to me, and I heard him for the first time.

I found out that one of the girls at the meeting attended my church. She told me about her involvement in the high school ministry I had never attended. I wanted to know more about Jesus and the real deal about my life and my eternity. Over the next couple of months, I consistently attended the high school ministry at my church with my new FCA friends. I started to read the Bible every day and learned so much about God's character and incredible love for me.

> "The Lord is near to all who call on him, to all who call on him in truth" (Psalm 145:18).

One day, my mom asked if I had asked Jesus to come into my heart yet. I said no, but I realized there was no reason to wait any longer to begin a personal relationship with him. I went up to my room that night and confessed my sins to Jesus and asked him to lead my life. It was the most significant day of my life.

Not long ago, my mom and I got baptized together at our church. I wanted everyone to know that I'm living my life for Jesus now.

What God Taught Me

• God has blessed me beyond comprehension. Life hasn't all been easy, but I've never felt alone since God has been in my life.

• God is the center of my life, and I want to be available for him to use me in any situation.

• I'm always going to be far from perfect, but God never gives up on me.

Write Your Story

How have your parents helped or hurt the shaping of your faith? Have they been a source of encouragement or discouragement in your relationship with God?

Talk to God

Use this prayer, or talk to God in your own words:

Jesus, you have shown me such grace and mercy! I want to grow closer to you and know you better. Thank you for meeting me where I am and loving me. I want to glorify you in all I do. Amen.

Talk With Friends

In a small group, talk about these questions:

• In what area of your life have you felt God at work lately?

• How has God been present in the midst of your victories and struggles?

• What do you think it means to honor God with your life? How can you take steps to do just that?

Looking for Answers
Todd's Story

Each year, every junior at my school has to write a long term paper. Unlike other assigned term papers, the topic for this paper is free choice. The only guideline is that each student must be totally interested in the topic. The teacher wants to make sure students won't mind spending hours doing research.

When the assignment was given, I started thinking about what I wanted to know more about. I had often wondered about the Bible and even questioned its validity. I had been a Christian for a long time, but I still doubted some of the basic truths about Christianity.

> "But as for me, it is good to be near God. I have made the Sovereign Lord my refuge; I will tell of all your deeds" (Psalm 73:28).

I knew I needed to fully believe in the truth of the Bible and its stories so God could use me to make a difference on my campus. I desperately wanted to accept all of Christianity's beliefs with my whole heart, so I chose to research this topic for my paper. I decided to prove the whole basis for Christianity. Many of my friends chose topics that they became bored with, but I never tired of researching Christianity. I was determined to find answers to all of my questions.

While researching, I regularly prayed, asking God to help me write the paper. I knew many non-Christian classmates would read my paper, so I wanted to find all the facts and share my faith with them. It was cool to learn more about the Bible and discover the historical evidence that supports the prophecies, authors, stories, and dates in the Bible. Through my time of questioning the details of Christianity, I found many answers and my faith increased.

When I became a Christian years ago, God touched my heart. Now God has touched my mind, and I can truly accept him in my mind as well as my heart.

What God Taught Me

• It's OK to have questions about my faith. I sought answers, and God responded by confirming my beliefs. Seeking for answers only made my faith in God stronger. I now have all kinds of evidence to back up my beliefs.

• God answered my prayers when I needed help in understanding the facts about Jesus' life.

• God is the center of my life, and it's my heart's desire for him to use me in whatever situations he brings before me. I don't ever want to be ashamed of my faith, but desire to be bold with non-Christians and show them God's love.

Write Your Story

It's OK to have questions about Christianity. The Bible promises that if we seek, we will find (read Matthew 7:7-8). What answers are you seeking so that your faith might deepen? Tell God here.

Talk to God

Use this prayer, or talk to God in your own words:

Jesus, you have shown me such grace and mercy! I want to grow closer to you and to share your love with my non-Christian friends. Please give me boldness and courage to do just that. I want to glorify you in all I do. Amen.

Talk With Friends

In a small group, talk about these questions:

• If you could personally ask Jesus one question about Christianity, what would you ask him?

• When you have spiritual doubts or questions, where do you look for answers? Who answers your questions?

• What would you say to a friend who doubts the validity of Christianity?

143

Nicole's Story

Even though I've grown up in a stable Christian home and I know all the Bible stories, I had never had a faith-building experience until recently. For a long time, I couldn't figure out why God would choose to love me. I had heard it a million times: Jesus loves you, he died for you, and so on, but to be honest I really didn't buy it. As far as love was concerned, my parents loved me, my grandparents loved me, and my friends loved me. I thought that was enough.

A few close friends and I started a tradition that stuck with us for years: We would write notes to each other and sign them "143." "143" stood for "I love you." "I" has one letter, so 1; "love" has four letters, so 4; and "you" has three letters, so 3—that's 143. It always made me feel so special when I would look down at the bottom of a note from a friend and see those three numbers. I was loved.

I also found love in a guy I dated for over a year. When we first started going out, it was awesome. We were perfect for each other. I thought this was the love I had waited for. But as our relationship progressed, we hit some rocky roads. We fought constantly and continuously broke up and got back together. I asked God to show me what to do, but I didn't seem to be getting any answers.

"This is how God showed his love among us: He sent his one and only Son into the world that we might live through him. This is love: not that we loved God, but that he loved us and sent his Son as an atoning sacrifice for our sins" (1 John 4:9-10).

One night, I came home late from a date with my boyfriend. The night had ended in a huge fight, and I was terribly depressed. The love that was so important to me was disappearing, and I felt as if my heart were breaking.

I lay awake in bed wondering what to do. Tears were running in an endless stream down my face. What should I do? Who can I talk to? Where will I meet my need to feel loved and accepted? In my moment of despair, I cried out to God. "God, help me. Please! I really need you now!"

Why did I feel like he wasn't listening? If he loved me, why didn't he show me? I tried again..."Lord, I need something from you now! I need you to *somehow show yourself to me, to comfort me. I need to know I'm important to you. Lord, I need you to love me."*

With tears fogging my vision, I opened my eyes and stared directly at my alarm clock. Guess what time it was? In bold red for me to see were the numbers 143. Right then, I knew God was there and loved me so much. He cared about my whole life. It was a faith-building experience that helped me give my whole heart to Jesus.

What God Taught Me

• God is interested in me and in all that's going on in my life. Even when he's silent, I know he's always there.

• I'm thankful I have people on earth who love me, but I know they'll disappoint me from time to time. God's love is limitless, and he will never let me down.

• God hears my prayers, even my cries of desperation. I'm working on praying not just when I need something, but also to praise and thank him.

Write Your Story

God is crazy for you! You are his beloved and precious child. How does knowing that God loves you help you through life? Is it simply head knowledge, or has it touched your heart? Tell God what you feel.

Talk to God

Use this prayer, or talk to God in your own words:

Jesus, you are love. You demonstrated the ultimate act of love by dying on the cross for me. Thank you for your sacrifice on my behalf and for showing me that I'm loved unconditionally. You're so good to me. Amen.

Talk With Friends

In a small group, talk about these questions:

• In what ways do people look for true love that only God can provide?

• What is different about God's love compared with that of the world? Is this true in your life? Why or why not?

• What are some examples of ways God shows love to you every day?

Trust Me

Mallory's Story

My health had never been great, so when I started getting headaches, it wasn't a big deal. The headaches would come only every so often and never last long. But then they began to occur more frequently, last longer, and hurt more.

Soon after my second semester started, the occasional headaches be-came daily migraines. They took away my ability to work hard at school and understand what I was supposed to be learning. My grades had dropped a little when I first started getting the headaches, but now my grades were plummeting. I knew there had to be something drastically wrong.

My parents made a doctor's appointment to see what was happening with me and if anything could help. The doctor couldn't prescribe anything or tell me what was wrong without doing some tests to find the cause of my pain. I assumed the tests were a waste of time and that I would hear, "Nothing's wrong. Take some aspirin, and you'll be fine." That's not what I heard.

I wasn't fine. Everything was not OK. The doctors found the cause of my chronic pain: I had a brain tumor! "Wait a second," I thought. "That isn't possible. I'm a sophomore in high school. Only old people have brain tumors!"

The doctor told me all I could do was wait, patiently and painfully, as my tumor grew to its full capacity. I didn't know what to say or do or how to feel. All I could do was cry. I don't remember how long I sat in the doctor's office and wept, but I do remember that at some point God was encouraging me from the inside. He reminded me that he was in control and that he works all things for good. How could God make any good out of this? I wasn't sure, but I decided to trust him on it. That was the last time I cried about it.

A few days later, I received a phone call from a neurosurgeon. He had looked over my records, and he told me my tumor could be operated on after all! Through that phone call, I could hear God whispering, "Trust me."

The next two weeks flew by with more tests, blood samples, and blood donations for my own surgery. They even shaved half my head. As the doctors were preparing my body, God was preparing my heart. "Trust me," he whispered.

The night before my surgery, I remember lying in my bed and praying, asking God to protect and heal me. I know God wanted me to trust him, but it was hard! It was my life we were talking about! But in the quiet of that night, I felt God tell me again, "Trust me."

> "Trust in the Lord with all your heart and lean not on your own understanding; in all your ways acknowledge him, and he will make your paths straight" (Proverbs 3:5-6).

I walked into my hospital room the morning of my surgery and found my pastor, my youth pastor, and other people from my church waiting for me. They prayed with me before I was wheeled into the operating room. The prayer time was incredible, and it gave me hope and inspiration as I once again heard God say, "Trust me, Mallory, trust me." I knew what I had to do: I had to trust God. I had to give him all my life, right in that hospital room. So I did. Not all my anxiety went away, but I felt good knowing I didn't have to pretend to be in control.

The surgery went great! I had to stay in the hospital for a week to recover because the doctors wanted to make sure everything went smoothly. Thankfully, it did. I was released from the hospital, but my journey wasn't over yet.

One side effect from the surgery was that I had to relearn how to keep my balance. I took physical therapy to learn how to walk again. It was so hard! But guess who was right next to me the whole time? God! And *guess what he was still saying? "Trust me!"*

I'm pretty healthy now. I can walk, run, and do whatever requires balance. And I don't have headaches anymore! My life hasn't been the same since the surgery and never will be. I've learned so much! God has been so faithful to me, and every day I continue to lean on God as he whispers, "Trust me."

What God Taught Me

• God provided people to support me through my time of need. I learned about the love of the church and how we can meet one another's needs.

• God hears and answers all my prayers, even if I don't realize it at the time. I know he cares so much for me and he can be trusted.

• Life isn't something to take for granted. Each day is a gift from God, and I need to thank him regularly for his goodness to me.

Write Your Story

We can forget how fortunate we are and start to take for granted all the blessings God has given us. Tell God what you're thankful for. Be specific.

Talk to God

Use this prayer, or talk to God in your own words:

Jesus, I am thankful that you are so trustworthy. You have never let me down. Thank you for your presence in my life and for being my source of strength. Help me keep trusting you with every aspect of my life. Amen.

Talk With Friends

In a small group, talk about these questions:

• Which area of your life have you lately been taking for granted: health, family, friends, material things…?

• What does trusting in God mean to you?

• What makes it difficult for you to trust God? What practical steps can you take to build your trust in God?

A Gift Just for Me

Kelsey's Story

During my sophomore year, I took a spiritual gifts assessment test to find out how God had wired me and what kind of gift or gifts he had given me. I cheated on the test. I didn't mean to, but I did. I answered the questions the way I thought I was supposed to. So my answers indicated the person I <u>thought</u> *I was supposed to be and* <u>wanted</u> *to be instead of the person I* <u>am</u>*. As you can imagine, the results were not my spiritual gifts, but the gifts I wanted to have. When I tried to use those gifts, things did not go well. I didn't feel very inspired serving, and I wasn't very good at what I was doing.*

Later that year, I started to serve on my campus team at my church's student ministry. I didn't know how I could help, so I asked my leader, Julie. Julie started me out with little things, like saying prayers in our team room, making phone calls, or setting up for our team meeting. As time progressed, I wanted to get more involved. The more I did, the more Julie trusted me to do. Eventually, I ended up planning our meetings each week and leading team events. I realized my spiritual gifts were nothing like what I had thought. I had the spiritual gift of leadership, which I discovered by trying things and finding out where I fit.

"Just as each of us has one body with many members, and these members do not all have the same function, so in Christ we who are many form one body, and each member belongs to all the others" (Romans 12:4-5).

I now try to develop my spiritual gift and use it to serve God as well as the people around me. I love using the gift God has given me to serve him because I am doing something I feel equipped to do. And it brings great joy to my soul.

The human body is a complex machine that functions only when all the parts work together. The hand can't write or pick something up unless the brain sends messages to the nerves that shoot down to the hand.

The same is true of the church. Every Christian has been entrusted with at least one spiritual gift to use to glorify God and to help the church function optimally. He didn't give you a spiritual gift to please yourself, but to serve other people. Discover what your spiritual gift is and put it into practice!

What God Taught Me

• God has given every Christian a spiritual gift to use to serve him and other people. Using my spiritual gift of leadership is so fulfilling and meaningful to me. I know I am making a difference for Jesus when I use my gift.

• God taught me how awesome the church can function when everyone discovers his or her spiritual gifts and uses them in service.

Write Your Story

Make a list of things you really enjoy doing. Look over the list to see whether you can serve God through each activity or talent. Ask God to give you an opportunity to use your gifts for him this week.

Talk to God

Use this prayer, or talk to God in your own words:

Jesus, please help me identify my gifts so I can serve you with joy and purpose. You made each of us unique, with different gifts, so we can come together as your church and honor you. Amen.

Talk With Friends

In a small group, talk about these questions:

• What are your interests or passions when you think about serving other people? Where would you like to see your life make a difference?

• What gift or gifts do you think each person in this group might have?

• What project could your group do together in the next couple of weeks to use your gifts to serve God?

Walking Away

Jamie's Story

I'm being raised in a Christian home, and I went through quite a process to finally realize that my parents' relationship with God doesn't get

me a ticket to heaven. I'm a pastor's kid, and I've tried for many years to not act or be treated like one. Although I gave my life to Jesus at almost every summer camp I attended, the enthusiasm never lasted for more than one or two weeks.

I wanted to go my own way, so I allowed myself to get drawn into the world. Smoking and drinking became normal, church attendance rare. I believed in God, but I couldn't feel or hear him. I began losing the values of my childhood and living a double life. My parents were worried and my friends wondered what had happened to me. I wanted to get out of the life I was living, but I didn't know how. I knew I was heading down a dangerous path and needed help.

One summer, I was invited to spend six weeks in Seattle. Never having been out of my hometown, I jumped at the chance to go. Deep inside, I hoped to find the way back to God, where I believed I really belonged. As I sat on the airplane, I felt a huge burden being lifted from my shoulders. Soon after I arrived, I met really cool people. I went to church without anyone forcing me to. I was having a great time, and I felt God working in my heart.

> "Cast all your anxiety on him because he cares for you" (1 Peter 5:7).

But two weeks into my adventure, I got a call from home saying my dad had been in a terrible accident. It was very serious, and the doctors said he'd be in the hospital for six months of recovery. All the small steps I had made toward God since being in Seattle were quickly undone. If God couldn't even protect my dad, how could he possibly care about me? I couldn't believe in him anymore.

I stopped calling myself a Christian and built a wall of depression, anger, and rebellion around my heart. I still went to church, but my heart wasn't in it. But God never gave up on me. One night during a summer retreat with the student ministry I was attending, I began to cry because I missed God in my life. I needed him to comfort me. I needed his forgiveness and love. I realized that he hadn't left me; I had chosen to walk away, and now I wanted him back in my life.

People came up to me and began praying for me. Suddenly, it was as if God were knocking on the defensive wall I had built to keep him out, and he said, "It's time to come home now, Jamie." In that moment, I tore down the walls around my heart and ran into my heavenly Father's loving arms.

Day after day, God shows me things to work on, and day after day, I grow closer to him and the person he has created me to be. What I figured was all just a bunch of boring traditions has turned out to be a living relationship with Jesus. My friendship with God is no longer a forced chore or a lifeless tradition. God is there every day of my life in the good times and the bad. And I am so thankful that even though I walked away from my God, he never walked away from me.

What God Taught Me

• God keeps on changing me. Life is about him and not about me, and a relationship with him is the most precious thing I can ever have.

• God is in control. My dad's accident happened for a reason that only God knows, and he knew how to work it out for good.

• God is never going to turn his back on you if you have accepted him in your heart. Whatever you have done and however long you have walked away from him, he is waiting for you, ready to forgive and to renew. You might not be able to feel or hear him right now, but don't let that stop you. Look for him and for the walls that might be standing between you and God.

Write Your Story

Take some time to read Luke 15:11-32. In what ways are you sometimes like the prodigal son? Thank God that he is always there for you.

Talk to God

Use this prayer, or talk to God in your own words:

Jesus, thank you for being a patient God. Even when I disappoint you or turn away, you patiently wait for me. Your love for me never changes, and I am grateful. Keep me on the right path and growing closer to you. Amen.

Talk With Friends

In a small group, talk about these questions:

• What kinds of people or things try to tempt you to walk away from God?

• Has there ever been a time in your life when you walked away from God? What circumstances contributed to it?

• On a scale of one (far from God) to ten (close to God), where would you place yourself? What would help you move closer to ten?

From My Head to My Heart
Ashley's Story

I've grown up in a Christian home where my parents' religion was passed down to me. I learned about Jesus, his disciples, right and wrong, and treating others as you want to be treated. I knew God was my creator and learned about Jesus' sacrificial death and resurrection. I felt like I had always known all that. So as I grew older, everything I had learned in my head seemed more like a tradition than an actual relationship with God.

I never had a life-changing event that led me to Christ. I had always been a Christian—like I was born into it. It was a part of my family. Sunday school and camps were all I relied on for my walk with God and before long, I began to wonder if God was even real. Church had become a chore, no longer a desire. I worried what my friends and family would think if they knew I doubted God even existed. I figured I needed to grow spiritually, so I joined student leadership in my high school ministry at church. I didn't really feel like volunteering, but I thought if I did work for God, I could figure out if he was real or not.

Months passed as I grudgingly set up chairs and tables for church gatherings. I wondered why I was doing these tedious chores. I was too stubborn to quit, but at the same time, I was completely miserable helping.

After I started volunteering, the leadership team had a backpacking trip for anyone who served with them. I had no desire to go and tried to get out of it. I really didn't feel like lugging a twenty-pound backpack through the woods with people who were so excited about serving a God I wasn't even sure existed. What if they found out about my doubts? What would they think of me? The only reason I decided to go was because a friend of mine begged me to.

The first night of the trip, my pastor gathered us into groups of three people we didn't know very well, or at all. He told us we were going to listen to the Holy Spirit while praying for the others in our group. I was hesitant and a little skeptical. I thought, "If God is real, he'll have to show himself to me." I was put into a group with two girls I didn't know at all. I wondered how they could pray for me when they didn't know anything about me. This would be a great test for God!

The first girl started to pray for my comfort in relationships with my friends. I couldn't believe it because the night before, I had been talking to my best friend about that exact thing! She even used the same words I had when talking to my friend. I was blown away! How could she know my worries and weaknesses so precisely? The same girl asked about my relationship with my brother, which wasn't going so well, and said she felt like she needed to pray for it and did. Again, I was amazed at the way God was revealing himself to me.

> "And without faith it is impossible to please God, because anyone who comes to him must believe that he exists and that he rewards those who earnestly seek him" (Hebrews 11:6).

It was time for the second girl to talk to God on my behalf, but she said she felt like she wasn't supposed to pray for me. Instead, she had seen a picture she believed was meant for me. She described a mother who greeted her daughter with a hug, only to have the girl push her away, run into the house, and stare out of the window, crying. That very scene had happened the day before with my mom and me. I couldn't believe it. It was as if God were talking straight to me through these girls. God was truly making himself real to me, a girl who doubted if he was even real! I was so thankful that God cared about me so much that he would take time to worry about what was going on in my brain.

The average distance from someone's head to his or her heart is *eighteen inches. I've heard people say that when you have God in your head but not in your heart, you're "eighteen inches away from knowing God." I had always known in my head that God was real, but because it had never reached my heart, I didn't always believe it. God isn't just a lifeless tradition I grew up with; he is real and living and wants to know me. That night I decided to close the gap between my head and my heart. I didn't want to be so close and yet so far from God anymore! My doubts began to quickly fade.*

I am so grateful that God would worry about the eighteen inches from my head to my heart. He wants to be close to you as much as you want to be close to him. You're only eighteen inches away.

What God Taught Me

• God is always there for me and always has been. God is real!

• Though not all Christians experience God in such a vivid way as I did on my backpacking trip, we all must realize that faith is the key to Christianity. Doubting God can stop us from experiencing his power in our lives.

• God can play an enormous role in my daily life. I give every day to him, knowing my life is in his hands. I trust him, knowing he wants the best for me.

• God used the power of prayer and the Holy Spirit to lead me back to him. Whether you're being prayed for or are praying yourself to experience God, he will reveal himself to you in some way. Just you wait!

Write Your Story

At one time or another, we can all have doubts about God. It's OK—God can handle it. In what ways are you doubting God right now? Take time to write out your doubts, asking God to strengthen your faith and answer your questions.

Talk to God

Use this prayer, or talk to God in your own words:

Jesus, help me know that through my times of doubt, I am able to get to know you more. Show yourself to me when I wonder where you are. Allow me the faith to trust you and to know that you're real in my life. Amen.

Talk With Friends

In a small group, talk about these questions:

- How has your family's faith or lack of faith affected your own?
- Have you ever doubted God? If so, what were the circumstances?
- In what ways do you notice the power of God in your own life?

God's Love Letter
Taylor's Story

Since I am a competitive gymnast and a high school senior, time is a scarce resource. I juggle a demanding schedule of advanced classes and homework, rigorous gymnastics training (five hours a day, five to six days a week), tutoring a ninth-grade student, various club meetings, college interviews, and church activities. I don't have enough hours in a day to do everything I'd like to do.

I often miss church services and Bible studies because I travel on weekends all over the nation for gymnastics meets; I am constantly turning down offers to go out with my friends, saying, "I have to go to the gym" or "I have a meet." So when a friend challenged me to read the entire Bible in a year with about twenty-five others in my student ministry, my response was, "There is no way I can read the Bible right now. I just don't have time. I don't even have time for what I'm already trying to do!" Reading the entire Bible was definitely something I wanted to do at some point in my life. Just not right now.

A couple of days after I had claimed I didn't have enough time in my busy life to read God's Word, I received an e-mail that said, "If you are too busy for God, you are too busy!" That hit me pretty hard. I realized God was speaking to me. I'm sure he had been trying to seize my attention for a while, but I had been moving at such a fast pace, I hadn't heard his voice. In the chaos of my life, I must have muted God's voice in order to focus on everything else that lay before me. Now I saw I had been neglecting the greatest friend one could ever ask for—the one who loved me so much, he gave his life for me.

> "All Scripture is God-breathed and is useful for teaching, rebuking, correcting and training in righteousness, so that the man of God may be thoroughly equipped for every good work" (2 Timothy 3:16-17).

So I decided to start reading the Bible. Because I had resisted starting for a couple of weeks, I was over a book behind. But I committed to doing it and asked a couple of friends to keep me accountable. What happened next is amazing: God not only provided me with the time to do the reading each day, but he also gave me the time to catch up!

God has been blessing me each day I read the love letter he sent to me. He's revealing to me his love, power, mercy, wrath, grace, and awesomeness. Once I joined the one-year Bible study, the excitement of learning about God rekindled the fire in my heart that had been cooled by worldly stresses. Now I can't stand to miss a day reading my Bible—it has become my source of strength, wisdom, and peace. This has been life changing, and I'm just getting started! I can't wait to see all that God will teach me through his Word.

What God Taught Me

• The Bible is God-inspired and true. It teaches us how to live fully for God.

• I was simply "waiting until later" when I had more time. But I need to adjust my schedule and give God the time he deserves.

• I sat in Sunday school classes for years and read excerpts from the Bible, but now I'm able to put all those pieces together, and a truly focused picture is appearing. God's Word has assumed a new power in my life.

Write Your Story

How well do you know the Word of God? How often do you read the Bible? What steps do you need to take to be more committed? Let God know your plan. Ask him to help you with this new start. Make a commitment you can keep. Keep the plan simple—try reading for ten minutes a day.

Talk to God

Use this prayer, or talk to God in your own words:

Jesus, thank you for the Bible, which is here to guide me through each step of the journey ahead of me. Help me remember your instructions as I live my life for you. But first, Lord, I know I must read the Bible to hear you speak. Please give me the dedication to do so. Amen.

Talk With Friends

In a small group, talk about these questions:

• What's your favorite book of the Bible? your favorite Bible story or verse? Why?

• How have you personally benefited from reading the Bible?

• How can this group encourage and challenge you to consistently read the Bible?

Clueless

Chris' Story

During my senior year, I faced the huge decision of where to go to college. My family and friends gave their advice, and I felt as if God were the only one without an opinion. I was confused because I wanted to do what God wanted, but I had no idea what that was. He didn't seem to be leaving me any clues.

My first choice was a small Christian college in another state. They offered an excellent music program, and I was impressed by their campus and academic standards. I thought I would attend that college, but God had a different plan.

"I will instruct you and teach you in the way you should go; I will counsel you and watch over you" (Psalm 32:8).

One Friday morning, I had an appointment with a representative from that college. He was coming to my high school to talk with interested students. I was psyched! My mom and school counselor came with me. But he got lost and was unable to meet me. I was really disappointed. Now what was I supposed to do?

My school counselor suggested that I look at an in-state school. She told me about an information day this college was having the very next day. She thought it would get my mind off my disappointment.

After some thought, my mom and I decided to drive to this in-state school and just check it out. The minute I got on the campus, I felt the sense of peace I was longing for. I attended the information sessions and toured the campus. One option of the day was a chance to apply to the college. I felt like God was telling me to do this. Within an hour, I was accepted and I just couldn't believe it! Just the day before, I had been so discouraged and doubtful of God's plan for my life, but he knew what he was doing all along. I just needed to be patient and trust him—something that's easier said than done.

My next big decision is to decide what to major in. I know God has it all planned out. I am just listening for him to guide me. I am confident that everything is in his hands and that he really does want the best for me. It's easy to get overwhelmed by all the decisions about my future. What's so cool about being a Christian is that God really does have it all figured out.

What God Taught Me

• I shouldn't doubt God's plan even if I can't understand what he's doing. God will never leave me alone to make a decision if I am seeking his will.

• God is always in control of the big picture of my life. He cares about my future and wants to be a part of it.

• I can put my trust in God, and he will follow through. He has a plan for my life, and he won't let me miss it if I continue to trust him each step of the way.

Write Your Story

What decisions are you facing in your life right now? How can you let God be a part of them? How are you seeking God's will for your life? Talk to God about your concerns, and ask him to be part of your decision-making process.

Talk to God

Use this prayer, or talk to God in your own words:

Jesus, thank you for loving me and knowing what is best for my life. Please help me put you first in all my decisions. I want to trust you with every part of my life and let you take control. Amen.

Talk With Friends

In a small group, talk about these questions:

• How often do you ask for God's guidance in decision-making? Do you just involve him with the big choices and forget to ask him about the little things?

• How are you actively listening to God? Has there ever been a time when you knew God's plan and did not follow it? Why? What did you learn?

• What concerns you about the future? How can this group pray for you?

Miracle in the ER
Jordan's Story

Who would have thought a regular day of snowboarding would change my life forever? I was on a church trip, having a total blast with my friends. On the last day of the trip, I was grateful for the memories we had made—and for all the incredible snow! On my first run of the day, I fell. I can't tell you what exactly happened because I blacked out and woke up face down in the snow.

I knew I was hurting, but I didn't think it was that bad. My neck was very sore, and my head was pounding. As I rolled over onto my back, I told everyone around me that I was fine. Of course, no one believed me for a second. I guess the tears dripping down my face gave away the terrible pain I was in.

After pleading with my friends, I attempted to finish the run. I soon realized that my pain was too strong to go on. One of my church leaders called for the ski patrol to come and take care of me. As they carefully strapped me onto the board, I was scared and shaky. My friends gave comfort and security as they prayed with me. I really needed them there for me, and they were.

> "Because of the Lord's great love we are not consumed, for his compassions never fail. They are new every morning; great is your faithfulness" (Lamentations 3:22-23).

As I laid on the board during the long ambulance ride, peace filled my heart. I had a feeling I was going to be OK, and I could feel God's presence right beside me. I was still pretty scared about what was going to happen next.

When I arrived at the hospital, I was greeted by my youth pastor along with two other leaders from my church. It was so good to see their faces. I really needed their support.

I was wheeled in for X-rays of my neck to see exactly what was wrong. The doctor told me I had broken my neck. I was shocked. I didn't know how bad the break actually was or what it all meant.

They wheeled me back into my room to wait for more X-rays. I was terrified, but I knew I wasn't alone. My friends grabbed my hands and started to pray. It was the best feeling to hear their soothing voices and to hear God speaking through them to me. I know God was there in our midst.

After our time of prayer, the doctors took a scan of my neck to try to distinguish the severity of the break. To everyone's amazement, the scan came back negative! The doctors were shocked and confused. They didn't understand this miraculous recovery. They took four more X-rays to make sure they weren't missing something. Again, the X-rays showed no sign of a break and no bone damage. I was completely healed!

The doctors couldn't explain it, but my friends and I could. God had heard our prayers and chosen to heal me—in more ways than one. He healed me physically, and also healed my heart and showed me how to trust him with my whole life. He gave me the knowledge and reassurance that he is all-powerful. I will never be the same again!

What God Taught Me

• God's power is limitless. He shows me in small and big ways how strong he is and how able he is to handle anything that comes my way.

• God continues to amaze me every day of my life, and I am so thankful. His ways are wonderful, and I am blessed beyond belief.

• I learned about the importance of good Christian friends. When I faced my crisis, they were there for me, praying and supporting me.

Write Your Story

Sometimes it's hard to believe that God really can do all he says he can do. But with God, all things are possible. Is there an area of your life in which you doubt God's ability to help you? Talk to him about it here.

Talk to God

Use this prayer, or talk to God in your own words:

Jesus, thank you for demonstrating your goodness and power to me. I feel secure knowing my life is in your hands. You have a perfect plan for my life, and I trust in you. Thank you for being so faithful to me. Amen.

Talk With Friends

In a small group, talk about these questions:

• Do you believe God heals people today? Do you know anyone whom God has physically healed?

• Why does God choose to heal some people and not others?

• Who do you know who needs God's help right now? Share those needs, and spend time praying as a group.

Only One

Jared's Story

After an early hockey practice one Saturday morning, I drove two of my hockey friends home. I relaxed for a couple of hours before going to see my brother wrestle in a tournament. On the way there, I noticed something seemed wrong with the brakes on my car. I didn't have time to stop and get them checked, so I blew it off and joined the flow of traffic on the freeway.

About a mile from my exit, I made my way to the right lane. I stepped gently on the brakes to decrease my speed. As my exit came up, I stepped on the brakes once more, but this time the van I was driving suddenly pulled to the right side of the road and onto the shoulder. Thinking I could correct the error, I tried steering back into the lane, but forgot to take my foot off the brake. The van rolled and went into an end-over-end flip. I closed my eyes and waited.

The van landed on its tail, and my seat buckled under the pressure. Even though I was wearing my seat belt, I shot out the back of my seat and broke the back window with the back of my head, landing hard on the pavement. While lying on the pavement, I heard a loud crash—my van had fallen off its tail right next to me. I opened my eyes and saw that I was two feet from the van and two feet from the lane of traffic. Fortunately, the first person on the scene was an off-duty paramedic. He took care of me until the ambulance arrived.

In the next twelve hours, I thought of all the "what ifs" that could have happened that morning. What if I had been two feet to the right? My van would have landed on top of me. What if I were two feet to the left? I would have been out in traffic. What if I hadn't been wearing a seat belt and had been ejected from my seat during the rollover? I realized God had been incredibly good to me. He was watching over me.

> "The Lord will keep you from all harm—he will watch over your life; the Lord will watch over your coming and going both now and forevermore" (Psalm 121:7-8).

I knew God saved my life, and I wasn't sure how to respond. Then I remembered a story in Luke 17:11-19 about ten men who had leprosy (a skin disease) and begged Jesus to heal them. Jesus had compassion on them, and their bodies were healed. Out of the ten, only <u>one</u> came back to thank Jesus for his grace and mercy. Can you believe that? Their bodies were free from disease, maybe for the first time ever, yet nine of them walked the other way.

I want to be like the one who expressed his gratefulness, not taking God's goodness for granted. I'm learning to regularly praise God for all the blessings he places in my life. My accident was a huge reminder to not be like the nine and walk away from Jesus. I want to be like the one and run to Jesus with a thankful heart, not just for the big things, but for his blessings every day.

What God Taught Me

• Life is precious. Every day is a gift from God. God spared my life, and I am eternally grateful to him.

• I need to take every opportunity to tell my loved ones how much they mean to me. Life is fragile. I don't want to have any regrets.

• My non-Christian friends need to know how much God loves them and how they can have a personal relationship with him. I need to share my faith and tell others how much God has meant in my life.

Write Your Story

When God blesses your life in some way, do you tend to be more like the one who returned or the nine who didn't? What can you thank God for today?

Talk to God

Use this prayer, or talk to God in your own words:

Jesus, thank you for the many ways you protect me. I put my trust in you and thank you for watching over me. You are so good to me and regularly bless my life with undeserved gifts. You are faithful, and you are my safe place. Amen.

Talk With Friends

In a small group, talk about these questions:

• What is one thing God has done for you in the past week that you could have thanked him for? Did you? Why or why not?

• How could you show your gratitude to God every day?

• Share a situation in which you would have made a huge mistake if you had not listened to God's advice.

A World of Difference

Alyssa's Story

Stepping onto the plane, I didn't know what to expect. "God," I prayed, "I know you put me on this plane for a reason. Show me what you want me to learn, and use my life for your glory." I was headed to the Dominican Republic, a Spanish-speaking country east of Haiti, on a mission trip with other students from my church. It was my first opportunity to serve God in another culture, and I knew I'd see incredible poverty in this Third-World country. How could God use me, an upper middle-class suburban girl, to relate and reach out to people who probably had never even seen a TV? I wasn't sure what I could even talk to them about.

For several years, I had enjoyed serving God in my church, but I thought this was a chance to take a big step out of my comfort zone. But after spending a week roughing it, using outhouses, and eating lots of rice, it felt more like stepping into my comfort zone.

"Therefore, my dear brothers, stand firm. Let nothing move you. Always give yourselves fully to the work of the Lord, because you know that your labor in the Lord is not in vain" (1 Corinthians 15:58).

Through the bond we shared in Christ, I was able to relate to many of the Dominican people in ways I never thought possible. We had more in common than I had guessed. Their smiling faces and friendliness drew me to them like a moth to a flame.

And their devotion to God was truly inspiring. I could see his love in how the people lived with such joy, even though they had so few modern conveniences or material things. Barefoot and modestly dressed, most families I met lived in one-room houses, yet I never heard a single complaint. They were the most content people I had ever met!

The Dominican people taught me many lessons about life, generosity, love for family and friends, and contentment. I was convicted to keep my life in perspective and not freak out when I can't find the right outfit at the Gap or the video I want to rent is unavailable. Things the Dominican people would consider ultimate luxuries, like new clothes and VCRs, I take for granted and forget to thank God for. I have so much to be grateful for!

Through serving, I found something I love to do: encourage people and show them God's love. I feel so close to God when I serve him with the spiritual gifts he has given to me. I'm still in the process of learning more about spiritual gifts, but this mission trip gave me a glimpse of what I have a passion for and how God might use me in the future to glorify him. What I thought might be a week of culture shock and exhausting work, God turned into a great adventure and one of the most life-changing weeks of my life.

What God Taught Me

• I truly felt God there with me. He taught me how to fully experience him in a very real way.

• God is not limited to the United States! My worldview was enlarged as I recognized the incredible bond all Christians share.

• I am blessed. God has given me so much and allowed me to live a pretty comfortable life. My heart is grateful.

• God taught me how fulfilling and satisfying it is to serve him. My life now has greater purpose as I use my spiritual gifts to make a difference for him.

Write Your Story

For what area of the world, people group, or social cause do you feel compassion? How could God use you to make a difference?

Talk to God

Use this prayer, or talk to God in your own words:

Jesus, what a privilege it is to serve you and to show your love to people from all cultures. I want the world to know of your amazing grace! Please give me an opportunity to serve on a missions trip someday so my relationship with you can grow stronger and my heart for people can expand. Amen.

Talk With Friends

In a small group, talk about these questions:

• Have you ever served God on a missions trip? If so, what was the highlight? If not, would you serve if an opportunity came your way? Why or why not?

• We can all lose perspective on how fortunate we really are. What would help you stay thankful for what God has given you?

• How could this group reach out to someone in need?

HOME LIFE

Joy in the Midst of Sorrow
Amanda's Story

My car lay in the middle of the road. Broken glass lay shattered on the pavement. My face was bloody and bruised. My lungs were struggling to breathe. There were loud sirens and bright flashing lights. "Oh God, no, please, God, no..." I prayed desperately as I sat in my wrecked car. I was sobbing and shaking. My mind was filled with fears and questions. Why was this happening? How could God allow this? Why was the Evil One trying so desperately to destroy my family? Could my mom take anymore? Could I take anymore?

For months prior to this accident, my family had seen its share of hard times. One of my brothers was in constant pain. For over a year he had suffered through countless surgeries. He tried to be tough, but we all knew the pain was getting to be more than he could handle.

At the same time, something even more painful was going on. My dad—my faithful, protective, humble, selfless father—left my family to have an affair. He left a life of love and happiness with a faithful, Christlike wife of seventeen years and four children for a superficial, lustful relationship with another woman. My life had gone from picture perfect to painful in one night.

My whole family tried to talk my dad out of leaving. We spoke long into many nights, shared Bible verses, cried, pleaded, and prayed, but nothing could break through to my dad. He was set in his decision, adamant that life with this other woman was better. He took everything he had taught us and threw it out the window. Our trust and respect crumbled. I felt betrayed, lied to, and abandoned. How could God ever heal all my hurts?

Nothing huge had happened before to test my faith. My relationship with Jesus had always been so fulfilling, so joy-giving, so steady that I wanted to share it with everybody, but now it seemed like someone was trying to steal all that happiness away. I wanted my old life back; I didn't want to go through any more trials. I wanted to grow in Christ through happy experiences, not ones that hurt so much. Why did all this have to be happening?

In my wrecked car, I had tears streaming down my face. I thought about my family and how they would feel when they found out about the accident. I wondered if we would all be OK, if we could get through everything. I thought about my mom—would this send her over the edge? My body couldn't move, but my insides were frantic! I needed to stay calm, but all I could do was panic.

Just at the peak of my freaking out, a man leaned his head through the broken window of the passenger side of my car. With a tender voice, he reached out his hand and asked, "Can I pray for you?" I asked him if he was a Christian, and he replied yes. The man prayed powerfully, asking God to protect me, to be with my family, and to give me peace. It was like the man was reading my thoughts. Everything he was praying for, I needed. Instantly, a peace that I can hardly describe swept over me. I began to relax and stopped crying. I opened my eyes to thank the man, but he was gone. I don't know who the man was or where he went, but I like to think that God sent me an angel.

> "God is our refuge and strength, an ever-present help in trouble" (Psalm 46:1).

After my accident, many friends visited me in the hospital and at home. Every time someone walked in to greet me, it was as if God were sending me another angel to care for me. I was facing a trial, but how could I lose my joy when God kept sending me tangible reminders of how much he loved me?

My dad is still hardhearted, but my faith in Jesus leads me to pray for his return to the heavenly Father and to my family. My brother is still in pain, but God is carrying us through that, too. My heart still hurts, but it is not broken. Life isn't easy, but I'm learning to trust. I now understand that hard times happen because we live in a sin-scarred world. In the midst of those situations, God gives us the opportunity to grow and draw closer to him. I have also learned to have joy in the midst of sorrow. God can use anything for his good. No one ever said being a Christian means that life *goes smoothly. But if you're a Christian, when hard times come—and they will—God will be right next to you. He may even send a few angels your way.*

What God Taught Me

• God is faithful. He doesn't break his promises. Even when I face trials, I can be at peace, knowing God has all my life under his care.

• God has taught me about real joy in spite of the trials I face. I've learned that happiness is temporary and is based on what happens or doesn't happen. But joy is not circumstantial; it is eternal and comes from God.

• God has taught me the truth of James 4:8a: "Come near to God and he will come near to you." When I spend time with Jesus, his presence becomes very real to me and I feel connected to him. I know he is always there.

Write Your Story

How has God been your refuge and strength during trials in your life? Give God thanks for his faithfulness, and let him know where you need his help today.

Talk to God

Use this prayer, or talk to God in your own words:

Jesus, I know being a Christian doesn't guarantee that life will be easy. Trials will come my way. Thank you for giving me strength and wisdom and for being by my side when I face challenges. You are so faithful. Amen.

Talk With Friends

In a small group, talk about these questions:

• Can you think of a recent time God filled your heart with joy or peace? How did it make you feel?

• In what area of your life do you currently face a trial?

• How can the members of this group support one another? What specific things can we do this week to make sure it happens?

The Royal Adventure

Melissa's Story

When I was fourteen years old, my family moved from Michigan to England. I hadn't lived anywhere besides my hometown in Michigan, so this move was quite a shock for me! I was dead set against going. After all, I had a good life in Michigan. I had great friends, a cool church, a big house—everything I needed or wanted was right there. I sure didn't want a life of tea and scones and people I had heard rarely smiled or laughed.

> "'For I know the plans I have for you,' declares the Lord, 'plans to prosper you and not to harm you, plans to give you hope and a future'" (Jeremiah 29:11).

As the moving date got closer, I started to question God. Why had he chosen me and my family to uproot and leave everything we knew? Into what kind of environment would he take us? Would I make any friends? Would he be there with me through it all? I had trusted God my whole life, but this was really stretching me. I was anxious to find out the answers to these questions.

After we moved, I started getting familiar with my new culture and eventually resigned myself to the fact that we weren't going back to Michigan. I missed my old friends and my old bedroom. But as

time went on, I began to learn things about myself and grow in my relationship with God. I began to appreciate a different culture and even started
to drink tea! I knew God was working in my heart and showing me that he
cared about all the areas of my life.

It took a while to find someone I could call a friend. However, over
time, God brought several new friends into my life. He has become infinitely
more real to me through all my uncertainty and doubt. All the questions I
had for God are getting answered in such cool ways. I'm convinced he cares
about my whole life!

I've been in England for a few years now and have not regretted the
experience. I've gone from dreading such a big move to enjoying all kinds of
new things and people. I have let God take control of all my life because I'm
confident he has my best interest in mind. He cares so much for me. I'm
thankful I moved—otherwise, I would have missed out on God's royal adventure for me!

What God Taught Me

• God taught me to appreciate life and the blessings he gives.

• God showed me on whom and on what I had built my hopes and
dreams. Moving forced me to rely on God, rather than on things or people.

• God will take care of me wherever I am. I can trust him with my
whole life and believe he'll provide everything I need.

Write Your Story

No one but God knows what the future holds. He has our whole life
planned out and wants us to trust in him each step of the way. How do you
feel about your future? What are you excited or anxious about? Tell God
about it.

Talk to God

Use this prayer, or talk to God in your own words:

Jesus, I can trust you. You have proven your faithfulness in my life again and again. Teach me to depend on you for all things. I want you to take control of every area of my life. Amen.

Talk With Friends

In a small group, talk about these questions:

• What is one of the biggest changes you've ever faced in your life?

• What role did God play in helping you deal with that change?

• Take time to pray for one another, asking God to give you courage to trust him with your future.

Prayers for My Father

Connor's Story

For some time, I knew my dad was an alcoholic and a drug addict. I could hear him lighting his pot pipe through my bathroom wall. I couldn't understand why he was doing this because he went to church every Sunday and claimed to be a strong Christian man. He had gone to a few Alcoholics Anonymous meetings, but they didn't seem to affect him in any positive way.

I prayed for him, but my prayers never seemed to be answered—until last summer.

We were on a family vacation, and my dad began to drink. He said he had control and I trusted him, but one beer turned into two, then three, until he was completely wasted. When he drinks, he turns into another person, kind of like a werewolf during a full moon. He becomes angry and violent.

That night, as my stepbrother and I were getting into bed, my dad and stepmother got into a huge argument. We were used to hearing them yell at each other, but this time the yelling turned violent and we heard three slaps and a slam. My dad had beaten my stepmother and thrown her onto the bed.

How could my father be doing this? As I lay in bed, I prayed for my stepmother's safety and that my dad would sober up and calm down.

The next morning, I had no idea how to handle what I was feeling or the situation I had been exposed to. I decided to pray that God would give me strength and help me get resolution to the pain I was feeling. But I bottled up all my feelings and didn't talk to anyone about my situation.

"Have I not commanded you? Be strong and courageous. Do not be terrified; do not be discouraged, for the Lord your God will be with you wherever you go" (Joshua 1:9).

After some time had passed, I finally broke down because I could not hold the pain in any longer. I talked with my youth pastor about what had happened, and I asked him what I should do about my dad's drinking and drug problem. He counseled me to face my dad, man to man, and to honestly tell him how I felt. That wasn't what I wanted to hear, but I knew I had to do it. I started to pray for the right time to confront my dad and that God would give me the words to say.

One Sunday night, I let it all out—everything. I told my dad I knew he was doing drugs, and I even told him I wasn't going to see him anymore until he cleaned up his act. He was shocked and angry. He couldn't believe what I was saying and tried to deny the allegations. But I knew the truth and kept telling him how I felt. When we finished talking, I broke down. I wondered if what I had done was right, but then I felt an unexplainable peace. God was telling me this had been the right time and place to do what I had done.

Over the next few months, my dad got professional help in a Christian drug and alcohol addiction program. He got sober and became an authentic follower of Jesus Christ. He is now very involved in the church and serving

God. We're still working on rebuilding our relationship, and it's been tough. But I know God is faithful—he's changed my dad's heart and mine. My respect for my dad is growing each day, and I desire to honor him like the Bible says. I'm confident God will restore our relationship.

What God Taught Me

• God is my perfect Heavenly Father. My earthly father will let me down, but God will never fail me.

• Sometimes God answers prayer in ways I don't always recognize at first.

• I need to continue to trust God with every area of my life. The power of prayer can change anything. With God, all things are possible.

• I cannot solve my problems alone. A mentor, small group, or pastor can provide me with guidance through tough issues I face.

Write Your Story

The Fifth Commandment (Exodus 20:12) tells us to honor our father and mother. For some, that's not too difficult (most of the time). But for others, it's hard to honor parents who blatantly dishonor God. How hard is it for you to honor your parents? How could you honor your parents this week? Is there anything you need to confront your parents with? Ask God to help you make the right decisions.

Talk to God

Use this prayer, or talk to God in your own words:

Jesus, thank you for leading me in life and allowing me to follow you each step of the way. You give me guidance from your Word and faith to trust in you. Thank you for your presence in my life. Amen.

Talk With Friends

In a small group, talk about these questions:

• How would you describe your relationship with your parents?

• Do you need to confront your parents with any truth about your life or theirs?

• How can this group hold you accountable to do just that and encourage you along the way? Be specific.

SOCIAL LIFE

Never Give Up

Danielle's Story

I had been praying for a friend of mine for about a year that she would accept Jesus into her heart and become a Christian. Every day I made an effort to talk to her about God, and I tried to be an example to her. When I did talk to her, I tried not to sound too "religious," but hoped she could see Christ at work in my life. Sometimes I wanted to give up talking to her because she didn't seem very interested, but I thought, "Christ hasn't given up on her, neither should I."

I kept inviting her to events with my youth ministry. She finally agreed to go to a concert with me. The concert was designed to let people learn who Jesus is and how he can change their lives. I thought it would be perfect for my friend!

I quickly called my Christian friends and asked them to pray for my friend. They all promised they would, and I was pumped, knowing my friend would be covered in so much prayer.

As we walked into church together, I remembered different times when I had almost given up on my friend and the words that had encouraged me to hang in there: "Christ hasn't given up on her, neither should I."

> "I tell you the truth, if you have faith as small as a mustard seed, you can say to this mountain, 'Move from here to there' and it will move. Nothing will be impossible for you" (Matthew 17:20b-21).

During the concert, we sang worship songs. I often looked over at my friend to see if she was participating, and she was! She was smiling, but I thought, "She's not going to accept Jesus into her heart tonight." But then I remembered, "Christ hasn't given up on her, neither should I." So I closed my eyes and prayed for my friend, who desperately needed God in her life.

We began to sing slower songs, and I could tell God was changing her heart. Then we all sat down to listen to a youth pastor speak. I was excited and nervous. I knew I couldn't give up now, so I continued to pray. My friend was listening intently to the speaker. Finally he asked, "Do you need Jesus in your life? If you do, raise your hand." I felt like my heart leaped out of my chest as I saw my friend's hand go up. I thanked Jesus for not giving up on her or me!

Everyone who had raised his or her hand was asked to go down to the front of the church to pray with someone. I asked my friend if she wanted me to go down with her, and she nodded. As we walked down the aisle, she turned to me and said, "I now see how real God is! Thanks for not giving up on me." I praised God that he had encouraged me to continue talking to her! That night, my friend began a personal relationship with God and gave him control of her life.

Over these past few months, I've seen my friend grow in her relationship with God. I'm thrilled to have been used by God to make an eternal difference in her life. It wasn't always fun or easy sharing my faith with her, but through it all, God taught me how powerful he is—he can change a person's heart at any time.

What God Taught Me

• As I interact with people every day, I should pray that they'll meet God and know him personally. I can show them God's love through my actions.

• God is there to help me through good and bad times. When I am weak, he is my strength.

• Many times, I was ready to give up on my friend because she wasn't responding to me, but God helped me stay faithful to her. His timing was perfect—much better than mine!

Write Your Story

The Bible tells us in 1 Peter 3:15 that we should "always be prepared to give an answer to everyone who asks you to give the reason for the hope that you have." How prepared are you to share your faith? Who could you share your faith with? Ask God to give you the right words and an opportunity to share Jesus' love with a friend.

Talk to God

Use this prayer, or talk to God in your own words:

Jesus, I want you to use me. Help me to have faith bigger than a mustard seed. I want to see mountains moved and my friends come to know you. Give me courage to share my faith. Amen.

Talk With Friends

In a small group, talk about these questions:

• How would you define "faith"? What does faith mean to you?

• Who could you share your faith with? Will you? Why or why not?

• What would help you be more confident about sharing your faith with a friend? What friend can the group pray for to come to know Jesus this school year?

Taking a Stand

Kyle's Story

In junior high school, I heard many stories about the parties, drinking, and drugs available in high school. People told me if you didn't drink or party, you'd be unpopular and have a hard time making friends. So when my freshman year began, I was worried about fitting in. I was soon invited to my first drinking party.

My first thought was to go, but my conscience kicked in and I said no, I wasn't into partying. The group that invited me shot me a confused look, and one guy finally said, "That's cool. I respect that." It felt good not to be made fun of.

> **"Be self-controlled and alert. Your enemy the devil prowls around like a roaring lion looking for someone to devour. Resist him, standing firm in the faith, because you know that your brothers throughout the world are undergoing the same kind of sufferings"** (1 Peter 5:8-9).

I was invited to a lot of drinking parties, and my response was always the same. As months went by, I noticed I wasn't being invited to many parties. Fewer people were asking me to get drunk or high. I realized that this wasn't because I was unpopular; it was because everyone already knew my answer. I was still friends with the kids who invited me to parties, and I hung out with them a lot at school, but they knew not to ask me to drink because I was going to refuse.

Some Christian friends think I'm wrong to hang out with people who drink and get high, but I disagree. I try to follow how Jesus lived his life as described in the Bible. He was friends with partiers and tax collectors and prostitutes. Jesus was frowned upon for visiting unpopular people like Zacchaeus, a tax collector. When people asked Jesus why he befriended sinners, he answered: "For the Son of Man came to seek and to save what was lost" (Luke 19:10).

According to the way Jesus lived his life, it's OK to hang out with sinful people, but not to give in to sin. My non-Christian friends tell me they're proud of me for not drinking and doing drugs. I talk with them about my relationship with God, and I'm showing them that life can be fun as a Christian. I try to be an example to them and pray that one day they will trust Jesus with their lives.

What God Taught Me

• It's OK to be friends with people who party as long as I keep my standards high.

• Not drinking or doing drugs doesn't make me unpopular. Most kids respect my decision.

• I need to continue to pray for and share my faith with my non-Christian friends who are caught up in alcohol or drugs.

• God regularly reminds me to pray that I will resist the temptation of drinking and drugs.

Write Your Story

We all face temptation to disobey God. In what area of life do you feel the most temptation? Ask God to give you strength to stand strong in this area.

Talk to God

Use this prayer, or talk to God in your own words:

Jesus, please give me the courage to stand for what I know is right. Help me to refuse the temptation of partying. I pray for opportunities to talk with my non-Christian friends about you. Amen.

Talk With Friends

In a small group, talk about these questions:

• What is your view on alcohol and drugs? How big a temptation are they in your life? Are drugs and alcohol prevalent in your school?

• How do your classmates view students who have chosen not to party?

• Suppose someone asks you to party with him or her. How would you explain your stand on partying? Would you still hang out with him or her at school? Why or why not?

No Turning Back
Megan's Story

When I was two years old, I was very independent. My mom would try to help me put my coat on or cut my food, and I would turn to her and say, "Megan do!" I wanted to do everything myself. My family would laugh about it and always tease me whenever I wanted to do something on my own by saying to me, "Megan do! Megan do!" That independent attitude followed me for a long time.

When I started high school, I bumped into Tyler, one of my brother's old friends. Tyler and my brother had partied a lot together. Tyler had done drugs and been involved in gangs, but when I saw him at school, he was a totally different person. He said he had become a Christian and had given up his old lifestyle. He invited me to go to his youth ministry and check it out. I was curious, so I went and was very impressed. I continued to go on my own. He invited me to a winter weekend retreat, where I heard about a God who loved me and had a plan for my life. It blew me away! During that weekend, I made the decision to start a personal relationship with God and trust him with my life.

I came back from the retreat totally pumped to go home and share my new faith. I was determined to stop partying and start living like a Christ-follower. But when I got back around my friends, I fell into my old ways of smoking, drinking, and doing drugs. I was having such a good time partying (or at least I thought I was) that I didn't want to give that up for God.

So I decided to push God away when I didn't want him around interfering in my life. Just like when I was two, I wanted to be independent. Without realizing it, I had turned to God and said, "Megan do!"

That summer I went to church camp. I figured I could take a week out of my partying schedule to get a tan and check out the guys. Well, camp impacted me more than a nice tan or getting a date. I went home on fire for God. I was ready to make a change. It wouldn't be easy, but I thought things were different.

As soon as I got home, I faced a test. A guy I had liked for four years asked me out. I knew he wasn't a Christian and he would bring me down in my relationship with God, so I told him no. I cried for hours! Some of the tears were from happiness, knowing I had made the right decision. Other tears were from sadness, knowing I had passed up an opportunity that would never come again.

I was determined to live for Jesus, but I didn't have a lot of Christian friends close by, so I got bored. I started hanging out with my old friends. I thought I could handle it, but before I knew it, I was partying every other night. First I just went to hang out with them, then the next time I decided to just have a beer and a cigarette. Before long, I was drinking, smoking, and doing drugs just like old times. But this time I fell in even deeper. I started going out with a drug dealer, doing heavier drugs, lying to my parents, and denying my faith in God. I could sense God offering his help, but my spirit kept saying, "Megan do!"

I don't know why, but I still attended my student ministry during this time. I knew I wasn't living my life the way God would want me to, but it felt like if I went to church, I could keep God a little happy. I ended up at a winter retreat again, and it completely impacted my life. More than ever, I was determined to change my life and to make it last more than a few weeks.

"Blessed are those who are persecuted because of righteousness, for theirs is the kingdom of heaven" (Matthew 5:10).

But what would be different this time? Would I just fall like before? Something needed to change, but what? Then I realized it! I had to change my life's motto of "Megan do!" to "God do!" I would let God give me the strength to change my life. I had been trying to do it on my own and was failing. This time I would depend on God and he would give me the courage to make it happen.

When I got back from the retreat, I broke up with my boyfriend and stopped drinking, doing drugs, and smoking! I cut off friendships with people who would send me in the wrong direction. It wasn't easy, and I couldn't have done it by myself. The only reason I was able to get out of this lifestyle was because I chose to let "God do!" I was learning to trust him with my whole life.

I took a lot of teasing at school when I broke up with my boyfriend. I had told him the reason was because I needed to find God again and have him in my life. He told everyone at school why we weren't together anymore, so people started saying things like, "Hey, Megan, I think God's at the end of the hallway. Why don't you go say hi?" or "Hey, you're going the wrong way—God's over there." A group of my old "friends" would fold their hands in prayer every time they saw me. I tried to laugh all of it off, but deep down it hurt me.

Sometimes I was tempted to hang out with my old friends, but then I remembered what happened every time I tried to let "Megan do!" I have been clean and sober for some time now. It hasn't been easy, but I know it's worth it. I still try to do things on my own, but I'm always reminded that if I want to be a true Christ-follower, I have to let "God do!"

What God Taught Me

• It's so cool to be able to stand up for Jesus, even though it's hard sometimes and friends don't understand my beliefs. I want to be an example to them and show them the difference Jesus has made in my life.

• God never gave up on me, even when I turned my back on him. He helped me get back up when I fell.

• God's path is challenging, but fulfilling and rewarding in the long run. The ways of the world can look appealing, but they leave us empty and un-satisfied.

Write Your Story

Life is full of choices. Sometimes we make good ones that lead us closer to God, but other times we take steps away from God because of temptation and sin. What kind of choices are you making these days? Tell God about it here.

Talk to God

Use this prayer, or talk to God in your own words:

Jesus, I want to make choices that honor you. Give me strength and wisdom to follow your ways. I want my friends to understand and know your love too. I pray they would see you in how I live my life. Amen.

Talk With Friends

In a small group, talk about these questions:

• Have you ever been persecuted or ridiculed for your faith? How?

• Do you have any friends in your life who are leading you astray and away from God? What changes can you make to stay strong?

• What temptations do you face in your life right now? How can God help you? How can this group help you?

Life's Too Short

Kerri's Story

I've always been good at helping other people resolve their conflicts. I can help them figure out what to say and how to say it. But with my own conflicts, it's a different story. Whenever I'd fight with someone, I'd withdraw from him or her. I'd stop calling or hanging out with him or her. I now have learned that leaving something unresolved can lead to a world of trouble and lots of pain.

Last year, my friend Brandy and I had an argument after a youth event. (I don't even remember what it was about.) We both left church that night angry and determined not to be the first one to talk. We went to school together, so we would see each other every day, but neither of us would even make eye contact.

The problem intensified when we began talking about each other to our other friends. Many hurtful and nasty words were passed back and forth between us via our mutual friends. All this talk eventually led to a full-blown gossip circle! Even though I knew Brandy was talking about me and she knew I was talking about her, we never actually sat down and hashed anything out.

> "If your brother sins against you, go and show him his fault, just between the two of you. If he listens to you, you have won your brother over" (Matthew 18:15).

One night during worship at church, I looked over at Brandy and realized how much I missed her. A wave of sadness and guilt swept over me—I had been so mean to her. I walked over, put my arm around her, and hugged her. She hugged me back, and we both cried, but we never actually talked—not one word.

The following week, Brandy and I were back to our old tricks. Some rumors started to spread, and soon our gossip circle had returned full force. My anger for Brandy increased each day and actually began to consume my spirit. My joy was gone, I was angry all the time, and it was wearing me out. (It takes a lot of energy to be angry.) All I could think about was how unfair Brandy was for not talking directly to me. I never even considered that she might think I was unfair for not talking directly to her. I got so fed up that I finally went to talk to my small-group leader about it. She suggested that I go to God in prayer to calm my anger, then go speak with Brandy. I prayed, but I never went to Brandy. We had been friends for over a year and I hated to see that wasted, but I wouldn't make the first move. I came to the point where I didn't even care if I lost her friendship.

All that changed with one phone call. A friend phoned to tell me that Brian, a close friend of mine, had taken his own life. He was fourteen. That day was a blur, between sobbing and phone calls from other grieving friends. I thought about Brian and how I never even knew anything was wrong. If only I could have been there for him. If only I could have talked to him. In an instant it hit me. I had some very important talking to do...with Brandy.

I picked up the phone and dialed her number. I told her the tragic news about Brian. She was devastated. I began to talk to her about the struggles she and I had been facing. I apologized to her for not communicating with her sooner. We both acknowledged that we had made mistakes and said how sorry we were.

I'll never forget the night I received the phone call about Brian's death. It always will be one of the saddest moments of my life. But I'm thankful that God took that tragedy and taught me that friendships shouldn't be taken for granted. We don't know what will happen tomorrow or even today. If you're fighting with someone, go make it right. Do it now! Life is too short.

What God Taught Me

• Friendships are valuable and shouldn't be taken for granted. A true friend is a gift from God, no matter how difficult he or she can be at times.

• I was too proud to admit some of the blame was mine. I looked at Brandy as a problem. I had to humble myself and admit my part in the conflict.

• By talking about Brandy to others instead of to her made me guilty of gossip. Matthew 18:15-20 teaches the right way to resolve conflict.

• God took a tough circumstance and brought the best out of it. He taught me how to really love another person and to ask for and offer forgiveness.

Write Your Story

What conflict do you need to resolve? Write steps to take this week to re-solve the problem. Ask God for wisdom and courage to make the first move.

Talk to God

Use this prayer, or talk to God in your own words:

Jesus, I know you want me to live at peace with everyone. Please give me a heart of compassion to sincerely love the people you have placed in my life and to deal with the inevitable conflicts in ways that honor you. Help me to let your love shine through me. Amen.

Talk With Friends

In a small group, talk about these questions:

• How do your family or friends know when you're mad at one of them? What do or don't you do to resolve the conflict?

• Read Romans 12:21 together. How can you try to overcome evil with good in one of your relationships?

• Do you need to tell anyone that you're sorry? To assure results, as a group make a commitment to keep one another accountable this week.

I Am Always Behind You

Brooke's Story

The week summer camp started, I asked God to help me meet someone who could encourage and challenge me. I didn't think it would actually happen. Justin was a bongo player in the student ministry band. All the girls thought he was good-looking, and I'll be honest, he was. But there was something more to him than just being fun to look at. He had God's love in his heart, and it showed.

Justin and I got to know each other at camp and decided to keep in touch. Like so many students these days, we found the best way to communicate was online. It was fun and it was free! As Justin and I talked online, the fact that he was good-looking disappeared. I no longer thought of Justin as the cute bongo player; he was Justin my friend, someone who could challenge me and help me stay on track spiritually. He was the friend I had asked God to help me find.

One day, after an awful day at school, I got online to see if my friend was there, and sure enough, he was. I needed his encouragement and advice. Justin asked how I was, and I completely broke down

> "As iron sharpens iron, so one man sharpens another" (Proverbs 27:17).

(as much as you can online!). I told him about my horrendous day, and he patiently listened. Then he did what I needed most: He prayed for me. Right there on the computer, we prayed! It was strangely comforting to read what Justin said to God on my behalf. Something he said in the prayer sums up what God has taught me through knowing Justin:

"I'm reminded of a story about a bear cub that was learning how to growl and fend off predators. One day the cub wandered off and a cougar tried to attack him. The little cub tried to roar, but only let out a little squeak. Surprisingly, the cougar ran off! The baby bear felt pretty good about himself. What the cub didn't know was that his father, a seven-foot bear with huge teeth and claws, stood up on his hind legs behind the cub and scared the cougar away. God is like the father bear behind us, guarding us."

God is always with us, watching over us and keeping us in his care. I'm so thankful he also puts people in our lives who care for us and stand beside us. Life is too challenging to do alone. I'm glad God and Justin are part of my life.

What God Taught Me

• No matter what, God is there to protect me and walk with me. He loves me more than I'll ever understand and doesn't want me to make poor choices.

• Christian friends can be a great help in living out the Christian life.

• God also reminded me of the power of prayer in my life.

Write Your Story

Reread the story about the cub and the cougar. Think about God's amazing love for you. In what area of your life do you need to feel God standing up behind you?

Talk to God

Use this prayer, or talk to God in your own words:

Jesus, thank you for meeting my needs so faithfully. You are a good and gracious God, and you have never let me down. I'm grateful you have provided people in my life who care for me and help me through life. Amen.

Talk With Friends

In a small group, talk about these questions:

• Do you have anyone in your life right now who helps you stay on track spiritually? If so, who is it? If not, how can you find such a person?

• How can you use e-mail this week to share your faith or to encourage a friend? Will this be difficult or easy for you to do? Explain.

• What would an accountability partner mean to you? What could he or she say or do that would be effective in helping you in your faith?

No Thanks

Jenna's Story

Have you ever gone someplace where you just didn't fit in? During my sophomore year, I was invited to my friend's eighteenth birthday party. She was one of the most popular girls in my school, and I knew this was going to be the party of the year that everyone attended. As an underclassman, I wanted so badly to fit in and be accepted by the older crowd.

The moment I walked into the party, my stomach became uneasy. I sensed that I shouldn't be there. I walked around the room, said hi to a couple of girls I knew, and tried to blend in. I saw a guy from my chemistry class. He came up to me, and we started talking. He was cool and easy to talk to. But then he offered to get me a beer. I had no idea people were going to be drinking at the party, and I felt really uncomfortable. I told him, "No thanks, I don't drink," and his attitude immediately

> **"Flee the evil desires of youth, and pursue righteousness, faith, love and peace, along with those who call on the Lord out of a pure heart"**
> **(2 Timothy 2:22).**

changed. He said, "Oh, I guess I'll see you around then" and left like I had a contagious disease since I had chosen not to drink with him.

As much as I would have liked to fit in, I wasn't about to lower my standards and go against the convictions God had placed on my heart. I knew I shouldn't hang around this group on the weekends, trying to be accepted by them, when they would bring me down. I remembered how thankful I was for the friends who share my beliefs and standards, hold me accountable, sharpen my character, and help me grow in my relationship with God.

I don't need a bunch of friends who try to find their acceptance and confidence from a can of beer, but I do need to pray for them and look for opportunities to talk about my faith with them. God can use me to reach out to them and to be an example.

What God Taught Me

• I don't have to conform to the standards of this world; I need to follow and honor God. I can be strong enough to resist the temptation to fit in. I shouldn't be concerned with what others think of me for my principles.

• I need to keep praying that I won't fall victim to an evil desire so I won't stumble in my relationship with God.

• God will use me for his purpose. He'll strengthen me so the next time I'm in a challenging situation, I can set an example and share my faith with others.

Write Your Story

We are bombarded with all kinds of temptations the world throws our way. It's tough sometimes to resist. In what area of your life do you feel God's given you victory in resisting temptation? Thank him for protecting you.

Talk to God

Use this prayer, or talk to God in your own words:

Jesus, thank you for giving me strength and courage to resist temptation and for giving me truth from the Bible to guide my life. Help others to see your love through me, and use me to make a difference on my campus. Amen.

Talk With Friends

In a small group, talk about these questions:

• Have you ever been in a situation in which you compromised your beliefs? Explain. What did you learn from it?

• What keeps you from standing up for what you believe in? What would help you remain strong?

• How can this group support you in keeping your standards high? Pray for one another, asking God to help you keep your commitments.

Baby Steps

Christy's Story

A few years ago, God put a challenge in my life I was totally unprepared to handle at the time. A casual acquaintance of mine, Kelly, told me she was pregnant. Since I didn't really know what to say, I went home and asked my parents for advice. At the time, my mom was pregnant with my little brother. That was good because I knew my mom could talk to her about pregnancy and baby stuff. I also started to talk to God about the situation and asked him for wisdom.

Kelly wasn't sure how her mother would take the news. The next day, I asked Kelly what her mother had said. She told me her mother was going to make her have an abortion. When she told me this, it broke my heart. I mean, this baby could possibly be the next president, or the scientist who comes up with the cure for AIDS or all cancers. But Kelly wanted to please her mom, and she decided to go along with the abortion. I kept praying for Kelly and the baby.

I did everything I could think of to get her to change her mind about the abortion. I told her that she would regret aborting her baby. I showed her actual pictures from a magazine of the stages of a baby's growth from conception to birth. I did everything I could to get her to change her mind. I felt God was leading me to keep trying to convince her not to go through with the abortion.

I called my student ministry leader, Angie, to ask her and others to pray for Kelly. When I told Angie about the situation, she asked me if my friend would consider giving her baby up for adoption. She explained that one of her friends had wanted to adopt a newborn for more than six years and would love to adopt Kelly's baby. I asked her to call Kelly and explain the situation.

> "For God so loved the world that he gave his one and only Son, that whoever believes in him shall not perish but have eternal life" (John 3:16).

One night Kelly called me in tears and told me she was not going to have an abortion. Instead, she was going to go through with the pregnancy and then give the baby up for adoption. I was so relieved and thankful to God.

When Kelly told her mom she wasn't going to have the abortion, her mom got very upset and kicked her out of the house. Kelly had to stay with a friend for the weekend until things could be worked out between them. Her mom finally agreed to support Kelly with her adoption decision.

The months went by, and Kelly's belly grew. Trying to keep the secret from the entire school got difficult because people were getting suspicious. Wearing baggy clothes was getting obvious. Eventually, everyone at school knew what was going on. Some kids were nice, but others pointed fingers and shunned her. I know sometimes she felt alone, but I tried to encourage her and be the best friend I could be. And God was by her side. She just didn't know it yet.

My family and I gave Kelly a baby shower so she would have some things on hand when the baby was born. It meant a lot to Kelly. I was glad my family reached out to her like that and gave her a glimpse of God's love.

The phone call I had been waiting for finally came: Kelly called to say the contractions had started and the baby could be coming soon. She ended up having contractions for three days, and on the third day, she went into full labor. Finally, she delivered a healthy baby girl. She chose my name as her baby's middle name because I had been a source of support throughout her pregnancy.

Once Kelly looked into her baby girl's eyes, she was convinced she couldn't give her up for adoption and decided to keep the baby. It was a difficult decision, and I wondered if this was the right thing for Kelly. But I continued to be her friend and walked with her as she adjusted to her new role as a mother.

After the baby was born, I started bringing Kelly and her baby to church with my family and me. Over time, Kelly learned about God's amazing grace and love for her and his free gift of salvation. It was an incredible offer she couldn't refuse. She decided to trust Jesus with her life and is growing in her relationship with him. I'm still walking by her side, but it's so cool to know that Jesus is, too.

What God Taught Me

• God gave me the opportunity to make a difference in someone's life.

• God gave me the chance to love my friend unconditionally, but also to see what could happen if I make the same poor choices. I have pledged to God that I won't give myself away sexually until I'm married.

• God can turn a difficult situation into a good thing. Kelly's daughter is a true miracle and gift from God.

Write Your Story

Does anyone in your life need your help? How could you show God's love to that person with your actions and not just your words? Ask God to help you keep this commitment.

Talk to God

Use this prayer, or talk to God in your own words:

Jesus, prepare me to be used by you, to do your will and to help lead people to you. I desire to show your love to those around me. Let my life be an example of your incredible grace. Amen.

Talk With Friends

In a small group, talk about these questions:

• If one of your friends were pregnant and came to you for help, what would you do or say?

• Together read Romans 8:28. In your life, when has God turned what you thought was a hopeless situation into good?

• Who would you turn to if you faced a crisis? As a group, thank God through prayer for putting those people in your life, or ask God to show you who those people could be.

Worth the Wait

Anna's Story

Our culture bombards us with the message that when we reach age thirteen or hit puberty, we're ready to date. I've grown up in a Christian family, and have an older brother and sister. Both of them started dating when they were thirteen. But I'm almost sixteen, and I've never been on a date.

Most of my friends are in relationships, and sometimes it makes me feel like I'm missing out on something really great. I'd love to be invited to a dance or just go to a movie with a guy. I've dreamed about what that will be like and who I'll be with. But in the meantime, I sometimes struggle because I don't have a boyfriend. Sometimes I feel lonely when my friends are out with their boyfriends. I think, "What's wrong with me? Why can't I get a guy to be interested in me?"

> "Every good and perfect gift is from above, coming down from the Father of the heavenly lights, who does not change like shifting shadows" (James 1:17b).

One night, when I was really discouraged, I sat down to read my Bible and came across Psalm 139. I learned that I'm chosen and I'm precious to God. God loves me so much and thinks I'm the greatest! He made me just the way I am. This was just what I needed to hear and believe in my heart. God's Word reminded me what's really true about who I am: I'm special and beautiful to God.

An older Christian friend reminded me that I don't need a boyfriend to feel loved or secure. God has a plan for me! Because of God's love and his speaking to me through the Bible and my friend, I found myself being more patient about dating someone, instead of acting so desperate. I'm becoming more secure in myself. I'm also more willing to let go of my life and trust God with my future. When it's the right time for me to date, he will make it happen. I feel so free!

Recently, I've been setting aside ten minutes a night to read the Bible and pray. If the prospect of a boyfriend comes along, I'll pray about it and trust God.

Ultimately, I know one day I'll find someone who God has planned for me to be with, and it will be worth the wait. Until that day, I know I am not alone because I have God by my side and that's enough for me.

What God Taught Me

• God taught me how very much I need to depend on him and trust him with every area of my life.

• I can't honestly say that this issue is always easy, but it's a whole lot more comforting knowing that I don't have to face it all alone. No matter what, I can put my trust in God and know he'll be there for me.

• God's love for me is awesome! The God who put the mountains in their place and created the stars in the sky loves me beyond my comprehension!

• My self-esteem needs to be rooted in God and what he thinks of me.

Write Your Story

Have you ever felt lonely or left out? Read Psalm 139 and take some time to write down what this Psalm means to you.

Talk to God

Use this prayer, or talk to God in your own words:

Jesus, thank you for being so powerful and in control of all things. I feel secure knowing that you have my life all figured out. Please give me faith to trust you with every area of my life. Amen.

Talk With Friends

In a small group, talk about these questions:

• According to our culture, what is the purpose of dating? Should this be different for Christians? If so, how?

• Should a Christian date a non-Christian? Why or why not?

• What does it mean for you to give control of your dating life to God? Have you ever done this? If so, how has it helped? If not, what prevents you from making this commitment?

TELL YOUR STORY

I hope you've been encouraged and reminded that you aren't alone. The stories you've just read are real-life stories from Christian students around the world who desire to grow in their relationship with God and who are trying hard to make choices that honor him.

You, too, might have a story that needs to be told, and I'd love to hear from you! Please send me your story so it can encourage others and possibly be included in the next student devotional.

Send your stories to:

Bo Boshers

c/o Willow Creek Association

P.O. Box 3188

Barrington, IL 60011-3188

If you'd like, you can e-mail your story to me at boshersb@willowcreek.org. Please be sure to include your name, address, and phone number so I can get in touch with you!

Scripture Index

Group Publishing, Inc.
Attention: Product Development
P.O. Box 481
Loveland, CO 80539
Fax: (970) 679-4370

Evaluation for
Doing Life With God 2

Please help Group Publishing, Inc. continue to provide innovative and useful resources for ministry. Please take a moment to fill out this evaluation and mail or fax it to us. Thanks!

● ● ●

1. As a whole, this book has been (circle one)

not very helpful   very helpful

1   2   3   4   5   6   7   8   9   10

2. The best things about this book:

3. Ways this book could be improved:

4. Things I will change because of this book:

5. Other books I'd like to see Group publish in the future:

6. Would you be interested in field-testing future Group products and giving us your feedback? If so, please fill in the information below:

Name _____

Church Name _____

Denomination _____ Church Size _____

Church Address _____

City _____ State _____ ZIP _____

Church Phone _____

E-mail _____

Exciting Resources for Your Youth Ministry

At Risk: Bringing Hope to Hurting Teenagers

Dr. Scott Larson

Discover how to meet the needs of hurting teenagers with these practical suggestions, honest answers, and tools to help you evaluate your existing programs. Plus, you'll get real-life insights about what it takes to include kids others have left behind. If you believe the Gospel is for everyone, this book is for you! Includes a special introduction by Duffy Robbins and a foreword by Dean Borgman.

ISBN 0-7644-2091-7

All-Star Games From All-Star Youth Leaders

The ultimate game book—from the biggest names in youth ministry! All-time no-fail favorites from Wayne Rice, Les Christie, Rich Mullins, Tiger McLuen, Darrell Pearson, Dave Stone, Bart Campolo, Steve Fitzhugh, and 21 others! You get all the games you'll need for any situation. Plus, you get practical advice about how to design your own games and tricks for turning a *good* game into a *great* game!

ISBN 0-7644-2020-8

The Youth Worker's Encyclopedia of Bible-Teaching Ideas

Here are the most comprehensive idea books available for youth workers. With more than 365 creative ideas in each of these 400-page encyclopedias, there's at least one idea for every book of the Bible. You'll find ideas for retreats and overnighters...learning games...adventures...projects...affirmations... parties... prayers... music...devotions...skits...and more!

Old Testament	ISBN 1-55945-184-X
New Testament	ISBN 1-55945-183-1

Awesome Worship Services for Youth

These 12 complete worship services involve kids in 4 key elements of worship: celebration, reflection, symbolic action, and declaration of God's Truth. Flexible and dynamic services each last about an hour and will bring your group closer to God.

ISBN 0-7644-2057-7